Praise for UX for Business

If you're a designer and not sure why sales/marketing/product wants to do X when Y is clearly better for the user, this is the book for you. Joel Marsh clearly explains the underlying value drivers for a variety of types of businesses (marketplaces, social networks, B2B companies, and more) in a way that can help a designer understand their stakeholders and the way to have the most impact.

—*Ellen Chisa, boldstart ventures*

If you want to know how you can impact business as a UX designer versus waiting for an invitation, Joel personally coaches you through this book on how to invite yourself to the conversation in today's workplace.

—*Christy Ennis-Kloote, Experience Director and Advisor, Latticework*

UX for Business weaves together concepts that drive value for both end users and business needs in a way that is easy to understand. It is a great resource for anyone working in a product company, especially if you are interested in getting a better understanding of various disciplines or different ways to think about business models.

—*Frances Close, Director of Product Design*

User experience design is broadly focused on user needs, but that's just one part of the equation as it should be combined with business strategy to also create value for the company. This book will quickly become a reference in the field as we cannot ignore any longer the need to connect UX with the business.

—*Kévin Meunier, CEO, Offinite*

Joel Marsh's book is unique because it covers the misconceptions and the challenges surrounding the user experience design, and especially in the context of new UX designers' expectations. It does a great job highlighting the discrepancy between theoretical knowledge and the practical realities of working in the industry and in the trenches from an expert perspective. There are few good UX books, but most offer quick solutions to becoming a successful UX designer, and often neglect the messy and challenging aspects of real-world UX design work. Marsh's book is one of the rare that aims to address this gap and it provides insights into navigating real UX design projects, in real companies faced with various constraints, stakeholders, and changing business priorities.

The book is organized into two parts: "The What" and "The Who." Part I focuses on understanding the different UX contexts and situations and adapting the UX process accordingly. Part II covers the challenges related to the stakeholders, and people involved in UX design projects, including UX designers. One thing that distinguishes this book from others is that it's anchored in organizations' business reality. Marsh emphasizes the importance of considering business and financial aspects and understanding the business side of UX work without compromising empathy and ethical design principles. He reminds new UX designers of the need to demonstrate their value by ensuring that they clearly align user needs with business goals: "User needs + business needs = Value." Very rarely do UX designers worry about value, and rather delegate this outcome to Product Management.

—Shaaron A Alvares, Senior Manager,
Organizational Agility, Salesforce

UX for Business

How to Design Valuable Digital Companies

Joel Marsh

Beijing · Boston · Farnham · Sebastopol · Tokyo

UX for Business

by Joel Marsh

Published by O'Reilly Media, Inc., 1005 Gravenstein Highway North, Sebastopol, CA 95472.

O'Reilly books may be purchased for educational, business, or sales promotional use. Online editions are also available for most titles (*http://oreilly.com*). For more information, contact our corporate/institutional sales department: 800-998-9938 or *corporate@oreilly.com*.

Acquisitions Editor: Amanda Quinn	**Indexer:** Potomac Indexing, LLC
Development Editor: Angela Rufino	**Interior Designer:** Monica Kamsvaag
Production Editor: Gregory Hyman	**Cover Designer:** Susan Thompson
Copyeditor: nSight, Inc.	**Illustrator:** Kate Dullea
Proofreader: Kim Wimpsett	

December 2023:   First Edition

Revision History for the First Edition

2023-11-30:   First Release

See *http://oreilly.com/catalog/errata.csp?isbn=9781098110598* for release details.

978-1-098-11059-8

[LSI]

This book is dedicated to my dad. The best diagnostician I have ever known.

Contents

The Who

Preface

Will You Risk It?

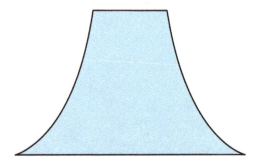

Imagine you are sitting on a motorcycle looking up at a huge ramp. The crowd is waiting. The engine is roaring between your knees. You may or may not ruin your underwear. In a few seconds, everyone expects you to jump that motorcycle to the other side.

Congratulations on getting your first job as a stunt driver! You earned it!

After reading all the books, doing all the boot camps, watching all the YouTube videos, and changing your X (formerly known as Twitter) profile to Aspiring Stunt Driver, you're finally here. But for some reason, now that you are here, you don't feel ready.

The ramp is bigger than you imagined. The crowd is distracting. The motorcycle isn't the one from the book, and everybody on your team has opinions about how you should drive it. The mechanics all wanted a *lighter* motorcycle, but the promoters wanted a *louder* motorcycle. You're driving the motorcycle that was "good enough" for everyone in the planning meeting. As you stare at the ramp and start to panic, you look to your coach for help. He smiles and yells, "We have a schedule to keep; just jump! Don't worry, the model we made says you should be fine!"

For some reason, that doesn't make you feel any better.

Models won't help you jump a real motorcycle any more than a user experience (UX) design course will help you solve real problems for real users. A model of UX work isn't real UX. If you lose your balance halfway up the ramp, you're still fu...in trouble.

It doesn't matter how it *should* work. What matters is how it *does* work.

During your first few months of real UX work, you will be in a meeting that suddenly feels like you're about to jump a motorcycle.

That's the problem that UX designers have today. And why this book exists. Everybody loves talking about how UX *should* work, but the only way to learn how it *does* work is to jump. But then, why did you read all of those books and do the boot camps and watch the videos?

That doesn't seem right, does it?

How Did We Get Here?

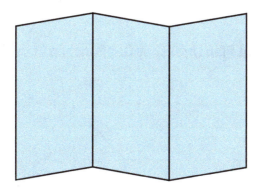

In 2016, I wrote a book called *UX for Beginners* (O'Reilly), because everywhere I looked people were asking, "How do I get started in UX?" At the time, I thought UX was at its peak, but I was very wrong. UX as a discipline went mainstream, and now it seems like every company that touches the internet—which is most companies—will eventually have some UX folks on the payroll. That book has become very popular, because it answered a good question.

Don't get me wrong, that's a good thing! However, a lot of entrepreneurial people noticed the demand for UX education, too, and unfortunately, they were more interested in money than education.

Since then, many courses, blogs, websites, books, and social media influencers have appeared, all trying to sell you the idea that you can get into this amazing world of UX design, where the salaries and prestige are high, and all you need is some empathy and a Figma account (neither of which are the key to being a good UX designer). And apparently, you can learn to do all these magical things in a weekend boot camp! Or a three-week course on Udemy! Or just by thinking happy thoughts!

Shockingly often, your teacher might be someone who makes more money doing courses than doing UX. Or the blog you're reading might be written by someone who learned UX last year, and they are pretty confident that they know how to teach others because that's what the boot camp certificate on their LinkedIn profile says.

One of the great things about writing *UX for Beginners* is that I've received many messages from readers telling me it inspired them to pursue UX as a career. It's one of the best things about being an author. But I quickly noticed a pattern: everybody wanted me to recommend another book that would tell them how to navigate their *real work*. Hmmm...that's a problem.

UX education—including books—often look nice in the brochure, but it's still pretty rough when you arrive.

"Everybody Has a Plan Until They Get Punched in the Face" —Mike Tyson

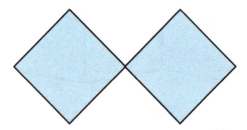

When you start working in UX, or switch to it from another career, you might be surprised when nobody else knows what a Double Diamond process is or when a design sprint doesn't magically solve all your problems or why "agile" UX is actually kind of awkward or when someone from sales or finance has opinions about your design but no interest in why you made your choices or when there is no budget for user research or when nobody has set up Google Analytics or when you have half the time you need to do a design and the requirements change in the middle.

Any of this sound familiar?

Someday, a fine person with good intentions will ask you to design the thing the developers are already building, which will just make your eyes roll back into your head and make you want to give up on life.

Nobody teaches you about that stuff, maybe because we want to pretend it doesn't happen, but also maybe because fewer people will take courses if they include bad news. Hmmm...

Most books and courses approach UX like it exists in a perfect world where designers are geniuses and everyone looks to us for whatever opinion we might have on our minds. I wish! It's a good way to *start* learning, but it's not the end. #designTwitter is all the evidence you need: it's more memes than expertise because they are more interested in attention than UX. Same problem.

In reality, you will work on various things, at different stages of development, in different companies, with different colleagues and company cultures that require you to adjust your approach without changing the fundamental principles of design. It is often useful to have the "perfect" process in the back of your mind, but with deadlines, budgets, sprints, meetings, company politics, and managers expecting great/unreasonable things from you, you need to be prepared to take shortcuts, compromise when it doesn't matter, avoid compromise when it does matter, make the most of the time you have, and make decisions with less information than you might want.

That's what this book is about. Real UX work at real businesses. All the messy stuff.

But it's more than that.

In all those workshops and boot camps and books, you might have felt like UX was just a huge collection of loosely related methods, techniques, philosophies, heuristics, and a bunch of other things you may or may not use and may or may not understand. Nobody ever really explained *why* we do these things. It was mostly just *how* we do these things.

When you go to work in UX for real, it isn't just design for design's sake. In many companies UX design can even be a luxury! You will care more about design than anyone else, which is a challenge. But also, you're getting paid! And that means that *someone* is expecting you to add *value*. Maybe even, God forbid, value that can be *measured*!

Value can mean a lot of things, and it certainly isn't just money, but money *is* part of your value as a UX designer. User growth, happiness, empathy, ethics, and usability all matter. That's what the job is all about. But if a non-UXer is talking about those things, they might use words like sales, lifetime value, competitive advantage, and return on investment (ROI).

Huh. The brochure didn't mention those for some reason.

To be truly *valuable* at work, you need to be able to understand the needs of the users *and* the business and design a solution that satisfies both. That is one of the first lessons in *UX for Beginners*, and it is a fundamental principle in everything you do as a UX designer. But it's easier said than done. That principle should be applied differently depending on *which* users and *which* business you're working with. That's not beginner stuff anymore. And! You also need to *sell* your design to your own colleagues and make sure it will achieve important business goals. Now we're in new territory. But that's the fun part!

To be an effective designer, you also need skills that don't look like "design." For many new designers, that can be a surprise like a worm in your apple (a reference to nature *and* technology!).

OK, Cut to the Chase: What's the Secret? (How This Book Is Organized)

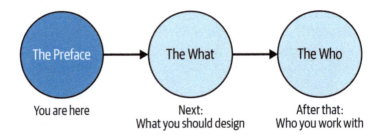

In UX, the right answer is often "it depends." Although the fundamentals remain the same, good UX *depends* on the situation. The secret is knowing *how* it depends, and that's how this book is organized.

There are two broad categories of "it depends" that you must understand: the *what* and the *who*.

"The What" (the first section of the book) is about *what* you should design. Is it an ecommerce store or B2B software? Is it a small, new startup or a huge, mature company? Is it an app for a brand or an app that should make money? Do users want to save time or kill time? Are you making a product from scratch or optimizing a landing page? And optimizing for what?! Clicks? Sign-ups? World domination? Different UX problems should be solved differently. In each situation, you could cause positive or negative results or might not make an impact at all. Do you know the difference *before* you start designing? After reading "The What" section of this book, you will. It contains many examples of how different design situations should change the way you apply the fundamentals of UX.

"The Who" is the second section of this book, and it deals with the people affected by your work. Users are definitely part of it—whether we call them customers, audiences, segments, or personas—but everybody teaches that part!

Users are not the whole story. The hard part is the people you *work with*. Clients, managers, designers and engineers, executives and finance people, sales and marketing people, and everyone else who might have the power to say no to you. We usually call them stakeholders. Ugh. It makes me shiver just writing it.

We will learn about researching, designing your process, and communicating with colleagues to ensure that they see what you see, and feel what you feel. As much as we can, anyway. No matter how much I love them, some backend developers and accountants are beyond the scope of this book.

"The Who" also includes the one person who will influence your work the most: *you*! Like any good kung fu master will tell you, you cannot master UX until you master yourself.

Wait, Go Back. What Was That About Money?

Yes, I said it. You have to care about *money* in this book. What? Blasphemy! Don't we design for empathy, purity, and nothing else?!

Let's unpack that a bit. You get paid to design, right? Or at least, you *want* to get paid, I assume. If you don't need to be paid, great! You may pass go and collect $200 and then give that $200 to charity.

But if you *do* want to get paid, here's a scary question: Are you worth it?

Companies do what they do to make money, at least partly. It doesn't have to be an evil capitalist conspiracy, although this book would be more fun if it were. That's just what a company is. Even charities need money! Customers pay money for something they want, and companies use that money to grow. If your company is on the stock market, the stock price will also depend on a lot of money-related things. So other people are thinking about money a lot.

"But we're UX designers," I hear you thinking. "Aren't we better than that?"

Kind of, but don't start polishing your halo just yet. What I am saying is: UXers can do more good by caring about money than ignoring it.

UX work isn't that close to the money, so it's not weird if you don't think about it as often. The finance department looks at the money every day, but you are mostly looking at pixels and people, so why should you care about money so much?

There is nothing "financial" about this book, but if your company is doing something good in the world, you should *want* your company to make more money. The path to success includes happy users and good products and smart insights and user engagement, but at the end of the day, those things are supposed to generate *money* so your company can do *more* of the good things you do! That's how your salary gets paid, why your team grows, where your budget for user research comes from, and the only way some people in the company will understand that you deserve respect.

Oh. Respect? Now we're talking!

The other reason you should care about money is that some people care about it *too much*.

It is extremely tempting for other people to ignore the needs of users or the ethics of design choices so the company can make a little more money or so they can get their bonuses, even if those choices will hurt the company in the long term. As UX designers, we can see these two priorities at the same time, and it's our job to show the "money people" the rest of the picture. But it is not always as simple as explaining the facts. You might need to speak in terms of costs or sales or risk to persuade other people in your company.

Every once in a while you might even have the opportunity to bend the *law* as a UX designer. Don't do it! But are you prepared to say no and explain why? Are you sure you would recognize that mistake as it was happening? Not everyone does. Dirty UX tricks can be tempting in the moment.

If you ignore the money (or its consequences), you might make bad choices or let bad things happen or accidentally destroy something! Being ignorant about your bad choices doesn't mean all of your choices are good.

You might miss opportunities to give users *more* benefits and value, because you didn't understand how money fits into the equation, just like the money people often miss opportunities to attract more loyal users because they are only thinking about the money. If you want to do the most *good* in your company, start caring about the money *and* the users at the same time. It will make you a smarter, more persuasive, more valuable designer, and allow you to get more of your (good, empathic, ethical, delightful) designs into the real world.

So, we need to care about money. It's not blasphemy. It doesn't ruin empathy. It's fundamental.

Why Should You Believe Anything I Write?

In UX, like in life, you should always question your information sources. What if this book is just a bunch of nonsense written by the latest AI algorithm, or what if I am one of those teachers who just learned UX myself?

I have been a designer since 2003. My work has been used by hundreds of millions of people around the world. I have worked on hundreds of products and services, ranging from startups of two people with no money to famous brands with massive budgets to complex ecosystems of many brands and products, in businesses that include everything from B2B blockchain-protected legal documents to communities focused on feminine hygiene products for girls. Today I run a firm of my own where we build software, analyze products and services for executives, and advise investors about how to spend their multibillion-dollar funds—using a lot of the same methods you will find in this book.

I'm a designer first. I write books when I see a problem that a book can solve.

I also have a bunch of senior product, UX, and marketing colleagues, who have been consulted during the creation of this book. There is a lot of real-world experience in the pages that follow. Not just experience gathered from other books and courses, but from really making things that were global successes, fascinating inventions, quiet failures, and a few that will remain ideas in someone's notebook forever.

I predict that the near future of UX work will evolve into something more like "business design" or "experience architecture." As more and more people become senior UXers, those people will see what I have seen: UX is in the middle of the business needs and customer needs that affect every aspect of a company's operations. From that spider-in-the-web perspective, it is often easier to see how an entire business could be made as effective as possible and where departments are not aligned. Sales, marketing, product, customer service, finance, tech, business development, and even the board of directors at a company are all trying to do the same thing, hypothetically, and a UX approach to the company itself—starting with the customers—is a highly effective way to think about a business.

That's what I do for a job. And that's why you should trust this book. But more importantly, that's why you should *try* the things in this book. They are battle tested and effective. This is not the brochure; it is the field notes from people who have lived with real-life UX for a long time.

But here is the real surprise: often your *best* work will come from projects that are difficult and messy, and your *worst* work will come from projects that are closer to the perfect world you were taught. Knowing how to work with real-world constraints makes you more *valuable.*

So, before you jump your motorcycle, let's learn some things you can practice first.

O'Reilly Online Learning

O'REILLY® For more than 40 years, *O'Reilly Media* has provided technology and business training, knowledge, and insight to help companies succeed.

Our unique network of experts and innovators share their knowledge and expertise through books, articles, and our online learning platform. O'Reilly's online learning platform gives you on-demand access to live training courses, in-depth learning paths, interactive coding environments, and a vast collection of text and video from O'Reilly and 200+ other publishers. For more information, visit *https://oreilly.com*.

How to Contact Us

Please address comments and questions concerning this book to the publisher:

O'Reilly Media, Inc.

1005 Gravenstein Highway North

Sebastopol, CA 95472

800-889-8969 (in the United States or Canada)

707-829-7019 (international or local)

707-829-0104 (fax)

support@oreilly.com

https://www.oreilly.com/about/contact.html

We have a web page for this book, where we list errata, examples, and any additional information. You can access this page at *https://oreil.ly/ux-for-business*.

For news and information about our books and courses, visit *https://oreilly.com*.

Find us on LinkedIn: *https://linkedin.com/company/oreilly-media*

Follow us on Twitter: *https://twitter.com/oreillymedia*

Watch us on YouTube: *https://youtube.com/oreillymedia*

The What

The Right Thing

How Do You Know You're Designing the Right Thing?

Wrong but comfortable	Wrong and uncomfortable	Right but uncomfortable	Right and comfortable

Before we talk about designing the right things, have you ever considered that you might be designing the *wrong* thing? Not just something bad. Something *wrong*: something nobody wants or needs.

Many designers have never really thought about it, actually. Sometimes we are too focused on which design we *like* the most, and we just assume the users will feel the same. Or sometimes we assume that what worked for us before will work again, so we copy-paste it and move on.

In reality, those can be big, expensive mistakes. It happens all the time.

Wait, wait, wait. If our favorite design might be wrong and the right design can be different from project to project, how do we know what to make?! What is this lunacy?!

The missing piece here is UX *theory*: the *reasons and principles* that make your design choices good, whether they are trendy or not.

Let's take this problem apart and see what it's made of.

UX Is a Process: Humans Are the Constant

UX is not what you do in Figma or a ticket in agile planning or the contrast of your button labels.

UX is a general process of designing things for *humans*.

Maybe you have heard: humans haven't changed much over the last hundred thousand years. Sure, most of us smell better now, but water, food, love, social groups, and high fives have always been important. Easy things are preferred over hard things; happy now is better than happy later.

We also think about our own needs more than those of others, because that is human nature. And that won't change while you are alive.

That is why UX exists. The needs of other humans are the non-negotiable part of our work. If we ignore them, we are probably working on the wrong thing. But when we understand the part we don't control—other humans—we can improve the part we do control: the business.

UX Is a Process: Business Is Always Different

Your second design priority (after the humans) is to understand the business. This is where a lot of UXers get lost, because they never think beyond the humans and the pixels.

Not only is every company different, but each company is changing all the time (some faster than others). Two companies that compete for the same customers will often have differences that matter. In fact, good business strategy *tries* to make your company different from competitors and change as competitors evolve.

That is partly why UX is a process, not a one-time task. If you aren't constantly adapting, you will make something based on old information, and it will be wrong. Or a design that was right before will become wrong as the world changes around it. And you have to do that without breaking the solutions for the humans!

Now that we have that covered, let's start identifying the right things.

The VDP Framework for UX in Real Life

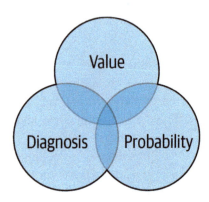

This book started by complaining, as I do, about common UX models that are too vague to be useful in real life. We don't need another one of those.

Instead, let me teach you a simple little framework that I use. It has emerged slowly from 20 years of experience on a wide variety of projects and works for marketing, product, and service design, whether you're using agile, Lean, or whatever.

The VDP framework has three critical parts:

>*Value* is created when your design works. Working means it solves a real problem in real life.

>*Diagnosis* is how you identify the problems worth improving, after your design works.

>*Probability* is a guide for optimizing your designs to squeeze every last drop of value from them.

VDP.

As simple as that might look, my claim is this: if you focus on those three things, in that order, using the methods I describe next, you will work on the right things in every project you ever do and avoid the wrong things at the same time.

Let's start with V for value.

Value

V = Value

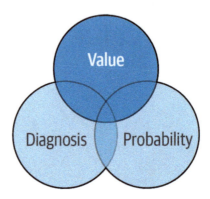

I understand if a *business model* doesn't feel like a designer thing. You're creative; you care about users; you want to be inspired. I get it. Especially if you are struggling with questions like, "What should I research?" or "What should I measure?" or "How do I get stakeholders to trust me?" Business models might seem off topic.

The irony is: the answer to all three of those questions is *the business model*, and if you're struggling with those questions, maybe it is because you think business models aren't a designer thing. (And remember: a lot of inspiring, beautiful designs actually fail in real life.)

Give me your attention for a few more pages and I promise to tell you how a business model can guide most of your big design decisions and make it easy to know what you should research, measure, and communicate to stakeholders.

But first, let's clarify something important...

User Needs + Business Needs = Value

If you're not creating value, you're working on the wrong thing. So, it is important to define *value*.

In *UX for Beginners*, one of the first lessons was about user needs and business needs. This is the other way we can look at a *business model*: it is the method of creating value for *both* the users (first) and the business, by solving or satisfying those needs.

For that reason, we care about customer problems and business needs whether we find them in data, user feedback, blog posts about our brand, or in a story from a tired customer service rep. Think beyond the screen!

Value is created by the *business*, not just the pixels.

Whenever I say *business model* throughout this book, you should think about *two kinds* of values: user value and business value, created at the same time.

Value Is User First, Business Second, and Always Both

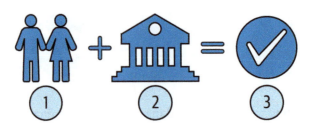

Every customer-facing employee has a story about a shortsighted customer or one of their unreasonable demands. Maybe for that reason, many companies talk about customers like they are an inconvenience.

In those moments, we act like the *business* is above the *customer*. We want *customers* to change to fit *the business*, apparently. That's dangerous. For *you*.

It's dangerous, partly, because customers are where all the money comes from! But it's also why I took time to explain that *people don't change*. If you *force* people to change, *you* become the problem. Customers solve that problem by leaving or choosing a competitor.

Customer needs and business needs are *two parts of the same thing*. They shouldn't compete. If the business wants to win, the laws of nature say the business is *never* above the customers. Businesses win by *serving* customers best.

Therefore, value should be created for users first, *then* the business.

OK, but Seriously, What Is a Business Model?

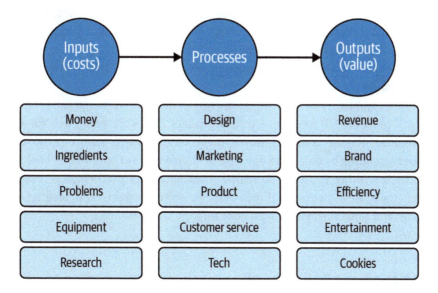

No design is an island. Design is just one part in a *system*, which includes lots of moving parts and people and processes that depend on each other. We call that system a *business*.

Like all systems, a business has inputs and outputs. The inputs of a bakery, for example, would include the ingredients for baking, equipment, employees, the physical or digital store, and the customers. Outputs would include the baked goods, the brand, and profit. Money is both an input and an output!

Some lingo: the money spent to run our business is our *costs* or *expenses*. Money from customers is our *sales* or *revenue*. If we still have any revenue left after we pay all of our expenses and taxes and stuff, that's our *profit*.

A business "model" is simply how all of the parts of the business work together (the design, you might say) to create value.

Value for the User, Not Lingo for the UX People

A phrase like "user needs" can be used to cover all manner of sins, so let me explain what it means before we get ahead of ourselves. You don't want to be one of *those* UX people who hides behind lingo.

There are two very general kinds of user needs, which I call *efficiency* needs and *entertainment* needs.

If the problem you're trying to solve for the user is based on efficiency, you will probably fail to solve it with the tactics that work really well for more entertainment-based needs. However, there are interesting ways to make effort more entertaining by doing the opposite, and we will cover both in this book.

The first thing you need to realize: user needs are psychological, but your design tools are functional. If you want to solve thoughts and feelings with features and functions, you should start with the user's mind.

Efficiency: Do More with Less

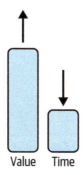

Value   Time

Efficiency problems are more rational than emotional, although solving them will give users plenty of positive emotions. They are solved by making things cheaper, faster, or more consistent (i.e., managing quantity, capacity, automation, data, productivity, and so on). For example, Google solves the problem of finding the right answer among billions of web pages by sorting those web pages in order of relevance. Excel makes it easier to sort and filter your information. ChatGPT writes content in minutes rather than hours or days.

When you design efficiency solutions, you should help people spend *less* time or money doing something, not more. Or make fewer mistakes. Therefore, you should measure the time, cost, or errors as your main metrics.

If you try to measure efficiency solutions with something like *engagement*, you're measuring the wrong things, because engagement is an *entertainment* metric. So, let's look at that now.

Entertainment: Good Feelings

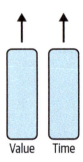

Value   Time

In this book, entertainment means a business that increases positive emotions (or reduces negative emotions), but it includes much more than the entertainment industry. If using something *more* makes people *feel better* (or if it makes money via advertising), it is probably entertainment.

Platforms like Netflix and games like Roblox are obviously entertainment, but for the average person, X and CNN are entertainment too. In fact, most of the top websites on the internet are entertainment, by this definition. Marketers might see X as an efficiency solution if their goal is to reach millions of people with ads, but that is why the "product" for advertisers is separated from the one used by everyone else.

To measure entertainment, measure how much time they spend doing it and how much they interact with it (i.e., engagement). If users play your game for 10 seconds on average, it's probably not very entertaining.

Later, we'll see that clever people can solve efficiency problems by adding entertainment value, but for now, let's just keep *efficiency* and *entertainment* as big, broad types of value.

Value for the Business: Efficiency

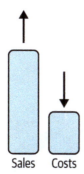

Sales   Costs

Regardless of what the user value is, the business cares about efficiency too.

The ultimate goal of any business is to create value at a lower cost than what customers pay for that value. In other words, the business wants to *make money*. That's an efficiency problem.

Your design might reduce the need for manual work, so employees can do more in the same amount of time. Or it might reduce the amount of data the companies need to buy to provide the service. Or it might make better recommendations to users so they stay longer and discover more things they like. Or it might make your product more unique, so you can charge higher prices.

Directly or indirectly, increasing revenue or decreasing costs is always valuable for the business, and therefore it is always valuable for you to think about.

Value for the Business: How Does It Grow?

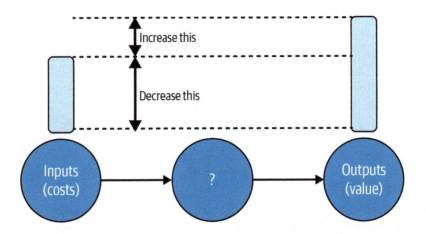

It's pretty hard to make something more efficient if you don't understand how it works. If you know how the inputs turn into outputs in the *business model*, then you will understand each step involved in that process. Don't just sit in your design cave and wait for inspiration; go out and look for efficiency!

How does each step add value? What are the costs (in time and money) to do each step? How can you design it so it produces more value or less cost, or both?

At the bakery, a recipe that requires fewer eggs is cheaper. If it is also delicious, then you have a good recipe design. If customers don't like it as much as you thought, then you need to try something else, because it actually *reduced* value. UX works just like that.

Map the process of making money as inputs and outputs, and the steps in between, and then look at the whole thing as something *you can design*.

Great. So, What Are You Making?

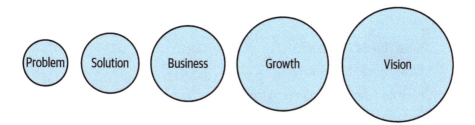

This is one of the first questions I ask entrepreneurs when I meet them: "What are you making?" Sounds simple enough, right?

Lots of people can give me the big marketing speech about making the world a better place or being the best such and such in the world, but few can describe what they are *making* and how it will *do that* in a concrete way. (Protip: If you have a job interview at a tech startup, ask that same question. If they can't give you a simple answer, don't take the job.)

At the bakery, we make cookies. But we also run a kitchen. We make orders for ingredients and receive deliveries. We have campaigns in the store window. And a website for catering orders. And *all* of that is what we're making. It's *all* part of the business model. Remove any part of that, and the bakery will create less value. "Selling cookies" is much more than the cookies. That's what we're making.

To understand value, and the business model, always start with, "What are we making?"

Let the Business Model Guide You

At the beginning of this section about value, I mentioned three common UX questions:

> What should I research?
>
> What should I measure?
>
> How do I get stakeholders to trust me?

Value is a big part of those answers. If you are trying to create value, then your time should be spent researching the business model. If there are issues anywhere in the business model that stop you from creating value, that is the *right thing* to work on. If nobody can find our bakery, maybe we need a new location, or a website with our address on it. Either way, there is no value without customers, so fix it!

That's basically what UX research is: finding issues in the business model (user value *and* business value!).

Once you understand the user needs and business needs—what you're making—you will know if it is an efficiency problem (less is more) or an entertainment problem (more is more). Measure the inputs and outputs and the business model process. Measure how much time and money users save (efficiency) or how many hours of good times they're getting (entertainment).

And then something magical happens with stakeholders...

When you have researched and understood the business model and know you're making the *right things*, and you can measure all the important clicks, costs, and conversions in those designs, you can tell your stakeholders exactly where your designs came from and how well they help stakeholders achieve *their* goals!

Value is the foundation of UX work. Now that you understand it, you know the difference between random "ideas" in a brainstorming meeting and truly *valuable* solutions in the business model.

Value Summary

Value is when you solve user needs and business needs at the same time. Usually that means solving a problem or creating positive feelings, in a way that customers will buy.

The business model is all the steps that are needed to create those two types of value at the same time. Usually, you can follow those steps up to one, or a few specific clicks or actions. Work backward from those moments and figure out everything that is needed to create value for both users and business, and design how that happens. For example, designing everything from when someone Googles "fuzzy hats" to when they click the Pay button at the end of the checkout in your fuzzy hat store.

When all of that works for the user and the business, you are officially creating value.

Next, we will learn the art and science of finding valuable problems to improve...diagnosis!

Diagnosis

"We Tried That; It Didn't Work"

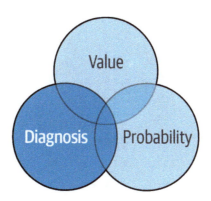

Ever hear someone say, "Ideas aren't valuable, execution is valuable"? Well, it's true. Designers usually agree with that. After all, we are the execution. You're welcome, everybody. But in practice, we also want to believe that all failures were bad ideas from the beginning. Otherwise, if the idea wasn't bad and it still failed, that means—gasp!—it was our fault?!

Don't tell anyone, but humans (even designers) aren't always perfect. Another good reason why UX is a process! If you design a good idea in a bad way, it might not perform well, people won't love it as much, the metrics will be uninspiring, and so on. Don't stop there! It was only your first version, so now your job is to design a second version. A better version!

The business model (value) allows you to know when something *should* work. But now we need a way to fix it when it *doesn't work,* instead of giving up after the first try.

Allow Me to Introduce Diagnostic Design

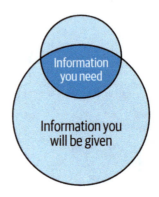

Many designers plan their work as if the goal is to get everyone to agree on a design. *Any design.* This is their plan:

Step 1: Brainstorm with stakeholders.

Step 2: Pick the stakeholders' favorite design(s).

Step 3: Ask stakeholders how they like their eggs.

Step 4: Swear a lot.

Step 5: ——

We want a way to design something that *works*.

As you become more experienced, you slowly realize that all UX projects start the same way. You are thrown into a bunch of information that you don't quite understand yet, including a lot of opinions that you might not agree with, and then you figure out what to make. Within all that information, some is useful, and some isn't.

It is that first, basic, hard problem of separating *useful* information from *not-so-useful* information where diagnosis will guide you home.

Diagnosis, generally speaking, means gathering information systematically, thinking about what we know, and drawing solid conclusions that are probably correct. We're *being diagnostic.* Thinking *diagnostically.* You get the idea.

Diagnostic thinking might not feel natural for designers who are more imaginative by nature, so let's start by using that high-powered imagination...

Imagine a Doctor

You walk into the doctor's office one day and confidently tell them you have some rare tropical disease, because that's what you found when you searched for "tired" on WebMD. You even bring up the web page where it clearly says that a symptom of tropical imposter syndrome is fatigue and after the last couple nights of binge-watching Netflix, you are definitely tired. And the doctor agrees that you look tired. Diagnosis confirmed!

Nah, not so fast.

You are wrong, and the doctor will hopefully find a better diagnosis...but what will make the doctor's diagnosis better than yours? Aside from about a decade in school and apparently several IQ points, the doctor will use a better method of *thinking* about your problem. They aren't guessing. They definitely aren't Googling around for "inspiration."

They are systematically thinking about the information they know and asking the right questions to gather more information. In that way, the UX process of deciding what to design and the doctor's process of deciding on a treatment are very similar.

Now Imagine *Like* a Doctor

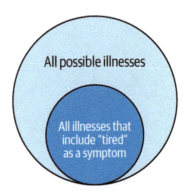

A doctor doesn't want to brainstorm ideas about what you *might* have. And they don't want to do a survey of other doctors or ask everybody in the waiting room if they agree. None of those people knows anything about *you*: the prob—uh, patient.

A doctor's mind is blank when you walk in. So far, no information.

You say WebMD says fatigue is a symptom of some nonsense. WebMD is irrelevant. But being tired is a *symptom*. That eliminates every diagnosis that *doesn't* include fatigue (i.e., you're probably not on cocaine).

But a lot of things could make you tired. Wait! See what we did there? We tried to *explain* the symptom and felt like nothing was an obvious *cause*. Also notice that we are not considering all possible ideas, only the ones that fit the symptoms. Cocaine is definitely out. That's a good start.

We need *more information*.

Take a History: Context Is Everything

In real life, if a doctor has never seen you before and you walk in and say you're tired, they will back up a step. They will ask about your general health and your family and probably listen to you breathe. What they are trying to do is understand the *context*. Doctors might say they are "taking your history."

If your mother has had chronic fatigue syndrome for her entire life, then perhaps that is related to your tiredness. Or maybe not. But if the doctor doesn't take your history, that information is invisible, so they can't use it to make decisions.

When a designer takes a history, we want to do the same thing, but about the context we're designing. We want to understand all of the general things about users, the product, the business, and life that might be big, relevant factors we should consider.

Ask Basic Questions First: Who, What, When, Where, Why

When you take a history, you don't need every little detail about everything. You're trying to get the information that means the most, and you can always dig deeper if you need that later.

As common and cliché as it sounds, the Five Ws are always a good guide.

Who are the users? *What* is this product solving, and what are we making? *When* does the problem happen? *Where* are they when they experience this? *Why* do people buy this? In my experience, the simplest fundamental questions are often the way to learn the most valuable, interesting things.

But also ask those questions from different perspectives. Who is the buyer? Is it the same as the user? What were you trying to do when you got stuck? When did you first hear about us? Where do you think you will go when you click that? Why are we trying to solve this problem for users at all? What happens if we don't?

You can go a really long way on simple questions!

Identify Symptoms

When you take the history, you might already get some clues about what to work on, but the real "meat" of the problem (or tofu if you're vegan) comes next: symptoms.

In real life, we usually don't know what the problem is, and we might not even know there is a problem! We're kind of assuming there is *something* that can be improved. What we need are clues to lead us to a valuable problem.

Symptoms can be something that "sticks out" in the data, like a low conversion rate or a common bit of user feedback or a feature request that everybody loves or a business requirement from stakeholders.

For now, we don't necessarily know what a real symptom is and what is just nonsense from WebMD, but that also means we don't ignore anything yet.

Never say no to new information!

How Do Symptoms Change Over Time?

The second part of looking for symptoms is to ask, "How do these symptoms change over time?" A low conversion rate might have started on the same day as the new ad campaign. That's important! But you won't notice that if you don't ask.

Or let's say you notice that a lot of users are deleting their accounts. A very serious symptom!

Is it getting worse? Better? Random? What if it started suddenly on Monday? What if other people saw it a long time ago and just didn't fix it? Or what if it only happens when a user does a certain sequence of clicks?

A customer journey document is one way to visualize how symptoms (i.e., experiences) change over time. It can also help tell that story to stakeholders. But the important part is to never ignore *time* as a factor in a diagnosis.

Make a List of Symptoms

This might seem basic, but even doctors learn to do this in medical school: make a list! As you get more experienced, you will be able to consider more things in your head, but even the most experienced UX people will document their research.

By making a list of everything that might be a symptom, you can step back and consider it as a whole. It is not just a bunch of random observations about your designs and your users: it is a list of clues.

Go down the list and think about what each symptom might *mean*. What could explain that symptom? What would make the data look like that? What feeling would cause a person to give such violent, rude feedback? What assumptions did stakeholders have when they made that request?

As you work through the list of symptoms, you might start to notice a "red thread" that symptoms have in common, which brings us to the next step in diagnosis...

Find Clusters of Symptoms

All of your intelligent observations share a context. The product or service. The users. The business. Therefore, we want to try to *group* symptoms based on what might cause each of those symptoms, or maybe based on when or where they happen.

If you have a request for a Save button and a request for an Edit button, maybe both of those buttons indicate that users are creating long content and they need more time to finish it before sharing? Those two symptoms might form a cluster of symptoms with a common, bigger cause.

Every time you can explain more symptoms with the same cause, that cause is more likely to be true! Whoa. Suddenly we're not just taking requests; we're identifying big chunks of value that we didn't capture in our original design!

That is the big idea with diagnostic design: find the biggest clusters of *related* symptoms.

Formulate the Problem

Here's where we turn observations into action!

When you have found clusters of related symptoms, imagine possible explanations of those symptoms. What is one realistic thing that might cause that cluster to happen? (If you have no idea, go get more symptoms!)

In real life, it is often possible to think of more than one reason why a cluster of symptoms might happen, and you should. The Save and Edit button requests could be symptoms of many things!

Each possible cause is a *hypothesis*.

A hypothesis is a very good guess that would explain all of your observations, the symptoms, if the hypothesis is true. You don't *know* it is true yet. You haven't *proven* anything. You just have very good reasons to believe that your hypothesis is realistic.

If you have more than one hypothesis, rank them in order of how believable they are. The most believable hypothesis is the one you will design first!

Test to Confirm (Ideally, with Real Users)

When the doctor learns that you also have a fever and a cough, suddenly you're not just a hypochondriac with a computer. Those three things are a *cluster* of symptoms, probably caused by a cold. *So, they run tests to confirm the hypothesis and to rule out more serious causes like pneumonia, the plague, or an alien parasite in your chest. Probably in that order.*

In UX, designs *are* the tests. We must design something that will work if our hypothesis is correct and will do something else if we're wrong.

For example, let's say nobody clicks our favorite button. Users say they love the page, want to click the button, and we're getting lots of visitors to that page, but still, no clicks. Sad emoji.

The simplest hypothesis: Maybe the button is hard to see? Good thinking! That would explain everything!

If that is correct, a big red button should perform better. So, try it!

More clicks? Nailed it!

No more clicks? Go to the next hypothesis on your list. You just learned something!

Hypothesis + Positive Test Result = Diagnosis

Remember when you thought you had COVID, so you did a rapid test, it was positive, and you swore a lot? That's what we're doing here, minus the swearing, probably. When you have a solid hypothesis and you do a test and the results of your test are consistent with your hypothesis, then you have a diagnosis! In other words, you have identified a real, valuable problem and verified the cause.

Sometimes you will actually solve the problem to do the test, like an A/B test (measuring which solution works better). Sometimes it will just get solid evidence about the cause of the problem, like in a user interview. Either way, now you are prepared to change your original design so it is improved *in the right way* to solve the problem.

A doctor prescribes medicine; you prescribe design changes.

After you launch the solution, follow up to make sure everything stays fixed. Measure it! A doctor will schedule another visit to ensure that the medicine made you feel better, and you should do the same with your designs.

You Are the Doctor; Your Designs Are the Patients

It can be tempting to think that users will tell you what to do if you ask or that collecting requests from users and stakeholders will be the right things to work on, but often they aren't.

Users aren't designers (lucky for you!), so they don't recognize their own problems. Even when they do, only the most obvious and trivial details are easy enough for a user to diagnose themselves. Same for stakeholders, but they are also biased about what is important. So, all that feedback really isn't a solution.

Treat all feedback and data as *symptoms*. Not hypotheses.

Write it all down. Consider the causes of each. Look for clusters with related causes. Eliminate possible causes until you find one that is realistic. But generate *your own hypothesis* in the end!

Diagnostic Design Comes with a Lot of Big Benefits

Diagnostic design *always works*, given time. Why? Because diagnostic design is a process that *eliminates bad ideas*. Every time you test a hypothesis, you learn more information. More information means *less* of your ideas will look smart. When you are totally lost and have no idea what to do next, the answer is: get more information. Understand your context better. Find more symptoms. Try to figure out what could cause related symptoms and *fix it!*

Diagnostic design is also the *cheapest* and *fastest* way to solve problems *that exist*. The hypothesis that explains the most symptoms is always your best bet, even if it turns out to be wrong. That means you are always working on the idea with the highest potential!

Remember: most ideas don't work. Narrowing them down to a few good ones is *extremely* valuable!

Diagnosis might feel slow at first, when you have the least information, but if you spend more time researching and developing a good hypothesis, you will move through the rest of your design process much faster. In a lot of companies, research is seen as the slow part, so some designers skip it and start making visuals as soon as possible. However, then you're building features that might be worthless, and it will take a long time to realize that. That's like a doctor prescribing medicine while you're in the waiting room. It might be the wrong medicine!

Although consensus-based design can feel faster because you get to start drawing sooner, over the course of a year, diagnostic design will create more value overall.

Another good thing about diagnostic design: it is impossible to work on things that don't matter. Impossible, you say?! Yes! If you do it right. Because you will only try to design a solution to symptoms that actually exist, instead of designing *ideas* that may or may not be useful at all.

Diagnostic Design Is Battle-Tested

This isn't some academic framework. This is science, and it is a proven way to solve unknown problems in the real world. Doctors have been using the diagnostic method since ancient Egypt!

Some people might call it *hypothesis-driven design*. I like that too. Diagnostic design is also pretty compatible with *lean* design, which is trying the smallest experiments possible as you look for a viable solution. Doctors are actually encouraged to only test for the information they need, which is a very similar attitude.

However, diagnostic design is not the same as *agile*, which is a project management method. A lot of people think agile makes a designer better, but it doesn't. You still have to plan your diagnostic work within your sprints if you want it to work. Agile can produce terrible designs too! Diagnostic design is also not the same as building consensus, which is when you get all the stakeholders to *agree* with your solution. We'll talk about that more in "The Who" section of the book. And diagnostic design is not the same as a "design sprint," at all. That's a week-long workshop for teams that have lost their way (and not the same as designing during an agile sprint, by the way...). Design sprints shouldn't be necessary if you practice diagnostic design.

On a Personal Note...

Diagnostic design is how I design. It is how all of my biggest results have been created. It is how I can be confident about doing something that competitors *don't* do and why I rarely have to look for "inspiration." It is how I find problems nobody else noticed and how I develop brand new ideas from scratch for startups.

I have 20 years of reasons to be confident that diagnostic design will make you a better, more efficient designer. But we still have one more big piece of the VDP puzzle to learn, because even a well-solved problem can be optimized.

Diagnostic Design, in Summary

Gather all of the information you can about your designs and the people using them. Feedback, analytics data, interview answers, online discussions, stakeholder complaints, etc. Make a list of observations.

Look for clusters of issues in your information that all seem to point to a similar or related cause.

Think of the *most likely* cause of those related issues (not just the symptoms!) and design a solution to that problem.

Test your newly designed solution in the real world. Measure it!

If your design created the improvement you predicted, good work. If not, use what you have learned and move on to the *next most likely* cause of the issues.

Repeat this process until it improves.

When it does improve, you're ready for the third and final part of the VDP framework: let's learn about probability...

Probability

Don't Be Lucky; Be Smart

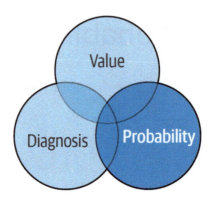

One of the most shocking things any designer ever said to me was that I was really *lucky* to get so many good A/B test results. I didn't know what to say. Instead, I started asking questions and soon understood that he thought A/B tests were a way to test your *guesses*. He thought I was guessing because *he* was guessing. He had no idea whether a new design would be better or worse and was relying on the A/B test to measure his *luck*.

Good UX is not a matter of lucky guesses. Guessing is not design. Design gets results intentionally. I hope, after reading this far, you are already starting to agree.

If you understand value in the business model and you have diagnosed all the big problems, there is one general principle that will ensure you get the most out of your designs: luck. Or the technical term for luck: probability. Your designs won't be better because you are luckier, they will be better because you understand how luck *works* in UX.

All Things Being Equal, What Will a User Click?

Instead of relying on luck, let's break down the behavior of one click to understand how it works.

Imagine a menu down the left side of a website, a very common design pattern. Maybe it is a list of eight different categories of fireworks. Which one will a user click?

If you don't understand probability, you might look at the categories and guess why one kind of fireworks will be more popular, or something like that. But I can tell you that statistically, *the first item in the menu is probably getting the most clicks.*

What?! But we don't even know what website we're talking about or which things are in the menu! How can we possibly know that?

Either I am a wizard or I just know how luck *works.*

Unfortunately, I am not a wizard.

Probability Intuition: You Can't Do the Second Thing Before You Do the First Thing

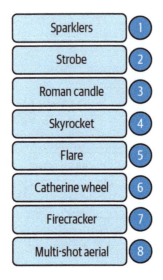

Let's deconstruct that one menu click and understand what happens in that moment.

Think about a user who *also* doesn't know which menu item to pick (i.e., every first-time user ever). They see a list of options, but do they see all of the options at the same time? Nope. They read the first one first, then the next one, then the next one.

Right?

And if they see a menu option that sounds like it might be the one they want, do they keep reading? No! In real life, they just click the first option that seems reasonable. So which item is seen by the most users? The first one!

When a million people do that, you get the most clicks on the first menu item, second most on the second, third most on the third, and so on. Because the only people who see the last item in the menu are the people who have *not* clicked all the other menu items on the way down.

That's probability. The *chance* of something happening. The chance of *less* people clicking more than *more* people is pretty low.

Effort and Time Both Work This Way

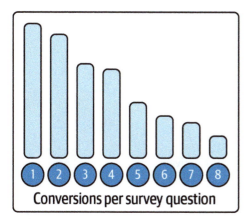

Conversions per survey question

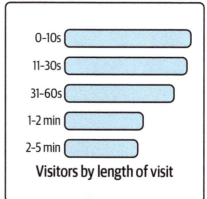

Visitors by length of visit

Imagine that we ask 1,000 users to complete a form. Will more people answer 5 questions or 10 questions? Similar to the menu example before, everybody who answers 10 questions has *also answered 5 questions* because you can't get to the 10th question without going through the first 5.

This is the reason usability exists. Because the less *effort* you need to do something, the more people will be willing to do that thing. It is a fact that more people will do less effort than more effort, because everybody who is willing to do more effort is *also willing to do less effort*.

One more example, to really make sure this idea is clear: time. In Google Analytics, one useful graph (a histogram) shows how long visitors stayed on your site. There is a bar in the graph for 0–10 seconds, 11–30 seconds, 31–60 seconds, and so on.

That graph always has roughly the same shape. Why? Probability, of course.

The bar representing the people who stayed for 0–10 seconds is usually the biggest. Even if a typical user spends 10 minutes on the site, they have to go *through* 10 seconds on the site first, before continuing for another 9 minutes and 50 seconds, on average. It is *easier* to spend less time than more time.

Incentives (Motivations) Also Work This Way!

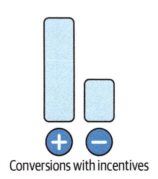

Conversions with incentives

Psychological probability!

If I ask 100 people to mow my lawn, a few ~~suckers~~ nice people might do it. If I also offer them a thank-you dance, more of them will do it (probably). Who doesn't want to see me do a thank-you dance?!

If we offer people good emotions or to relieve negative emotions, it motivates them. Or we could say it increases the *probability* that they will act. When we offer negative emotions, we don't get a lot of volunteers. In other words, it decreases the probability.

Incentives are simply emotional reasons to act (or not). Prizes! Appreciation! Fame! Exclusive access!

In UX we sometimes have the great power/responsibility to design incentives. No matter how many people would post on social media for rational reasons, more people will post to get likes and followers and feel good about it.

Likes and followers are features, designed by a UX person; likes and followers have changed the world.

"Yeah, but Who Would Do That?"

You don't need a deep mathematical understanding of probability to be a good designer. You just need a feel for it. We will see more examples throughout the book (which will make it clearer), but I want to introduce one more effect of probability first: the chance of a real user experiencing something.

The more users you have, the more often anything can happen. The opposite is also true. A 1% chance of a user deleting a file by accident might sound small, and if you only have 10 users, you might not see that problem very often. However, if you have 100 million users, an unlucky user is probably deleting their file right now!

Frequent usage also increases probability. If users work with files every day, it is almost a guarantee they will accidentally delete a file a couple times per year. What a pain in the ass! Once-a-year users still might do it eventually, but the chance is smaller overall.

A common debate in UX is: How many users do you need to test? It's only a debate because a lot of people don't understand probability. They think about user testing backward. When you do a survey, for example, you need a lot of answers because you want the results to represent a broad population of people. But user testing isn't trying to represent the population of users; it's trying to find the most common problems! Five testers are very likely to uncover any problem that affects at least 30% of users, because there is a high chance it will affect one of your five testers. The more you see that problem among five testers, the bigger the problem is! In fact, if all five users have the same experience, good or bad, more than 70% of *all* users will have a similar experience. The less likely the problem or the more accurately you want to measure something, the more users you need.

UX Is a Numbers Game

One way to think about UX is that we are designing and measuring *behavior*. UX, fundamentally, really isn't about the pixels and devices; it is about the way people behave in a designed environment.

Unfortunately, with so many users, so far away from us, we can't really *see* what everybody is doing. UX is mostly invisible in that way. Which is why we need to measure everything! Data makes UX visible.

For that reason, I personally don't think anyone can be a very effective UX designer without comparing the *visual* design patterns with the *data* patterns.

Data + Understanding Probability = Insights

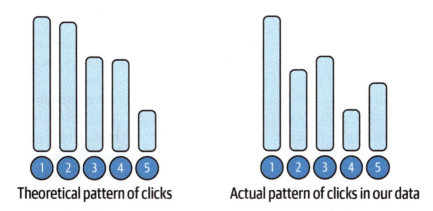

Theoretical pattern of clicks   Actual pattern of clicks in our data

With data, UX is suddenly visible, in the form of numbers. When we can see the behavior that our designs cause (think: symptoms), we can use that to improve our designs.

You might think, "I do UI design, so my UX is visible!" Not so fast, pixel pusher. Whether you designed it or not, visual UI designs only give you half of the information you need for UX work, and it's not the reliable half. Without data and user feedback, you're still guessing!

But data isn't the whole enchilada either. If we only look at the data, we still don't know what that data means. To close this information gap, we should always compare the visual UI designs with the data and user feedback to see if they make sense *together*.

For example, if your menu items are ordered 1, 2, 3, 4, 5 on the screen, but the data says the popularity of those items is 1, 3, 2, 5, 4, that's interesting! Are 3 and 5 extra popular, or are 2 and 4 not as popular as they should be? Since you understand probability, you recognize that the design and the data are "out of sync" with each other.

Like everything in the VDP framework, we need the user side and the business side to make sense *together*. Then we can ask why.

More Users, More Predictable

Your intuition might say that user data gets more complicated with more users, but actually no!

If your menu items are 1, 3, 2, 5, 4 in the data, but you only have 10 users, you can't draw any conclusions yet. One guy might click 3 and 5 every day and throw everything off because you're only measuring 9 other users.

Less users = less confidence in your data. Emotionally and statistically.

But with 10 million users, that guy can click 3 and 5 all day, every day, and it won't matter. The behavior of 9,999,999 other users will be so much bigger that guy will be irrelevant overall. Either the data will stabilize at 1, 2, 3, 4, 5 like you expect, or you can feel confident that 1, 3, 2, 5, 4 is the true order of popularity for your menu items.

More users also means more niche use cases, but we'll cover that later.

Probability Is How We Optimize

All of these probability-based principles add up to one big type of UX work: optimization. Conversion Rate Optimization (CRO) is a job title in UX for people who specialize in this type of design analysis. But even on products and services as different as B2B software, social networks, and games, the same principles of probability apply. We use them to ensure that we create the most value, as often as possible.

Probability isn't about making something work; it's about making it work better:

- Redesign menus, sequences of steps or clicks, and anything else that has an order to get more attention on the valuable stuff.

- Reduce effort and increase positive incentives to get more people to try or finish creating value.

- Measure the important stuff so we can see behavior and compare it to the data patterns we expect to see.

Suddenly, you might feel a little luckier!

Design Is Redesign: Your Second Try Is Often Luckier Than the First

When you approach design with your probability hat on, you will notice that the second time you design something it often works better. The reason is another consequence of this whole VDP thing: you can take advantage of new information.

After designing something, launching it, measuring it, and watching people use it, *you* now understand much more about your design than you did while you were making it. You have *more information*. Your diagnosis will be better, and you will realize where you can improve the probability of creating value. So, you will!

Design is a process, but not just a one-time process. We iterate! That means we do it again and again as we learn more. If you think your second version is good, wait until you see the genius ideas that appear for your sixth version!

There Is a Lifetime of Nuance to This

There are many other factors that combine with probability to determine what people will click. For example, a user must be ready to make a decision before they can make a decision. Sounds obvious, but if you have an ecommerce store, maybe the buy button shouldn't be on the first page. Users might not be ready to buy yet! Instead, it should be on the page where they first get the information they need to *decide* to buy.

Another version of UX probability is: How many users does a problem affect? Sure, maybe it is just a little problem, but if 100 million users will have that little problem every day, the numbers say it is a big problem! The lack of an Edit button on X comes to mind. It's not one typo. It's billions of typos. But there is a business reason (and maybe technical reasons) *not* to fix it, so they don't.

And yet another version of UX probability is, What is the default? If option A is selected by default, then you can bet your dog it will be chosen by more people than option B, which must be actively selected.

Probability is *everywhere*. We will look at more scenarios throughout the book.

You will need to research all the nuances of your users to understand which problems or opportunities should be seen by the most users, the most times, and have the biggest effect. But you can *always* trust that approach.

If probabilistic design doesn't work, you're probably ignoring the *real* probability that is affecting the user.

Probabilistic Design, in Summary

Using probability in design isn't always a purely statistical thing, like an A/B test or a survey sample size. Much more often you will need a sense of what is *more likely* to happen and what is less likely to happen.

Go through your design and consider how you have structured your menus, ordered your content, laid out your buttons, and how much effort and time it takes the user to see, find, use, or complete everything that is required. How many times will it happen, and how many users will it affect?

Make sure the most valuable actions and information are at the top, or first in the sequence, or the fewest clicks from where the user lands by default. Make sure the most painful mistakes are hard to do accidentally.

And think beyond the visual interface. Make sure good and bad feelings are aligned with the user value and business value you're trying to create. Efficiency problems minimize effort, and entertainment problems maximize good feelings.

VDP: Put It All Together

Make It Work, Make It Right, Make It Scale

I didn't come up with that catchy little phrase above. I learned it from smart developers. And if you have worked with (or read books by) smart developers, all of this VDP stuff might sound a bit familiar.

Programming is complicated. It is usually a bad idea to write a whole bunch of perfect code before you test that code. Sort of like designing a huge, expensive new feature before you talk to users. It's better to start small and test as you go.

Coders usually start with a "proof of concept" that is quick, ugly, and just enough to demonstrate that their bigger plan will, in fact, work. And at that stage, quick and ugly is great! When you know that it will *work*, you go back and do it *right*. You remove the ugly and do it properly, because now you actually understand what "properly" should look like. You fix problems. You make it stable. You handle edge cases. Well done! Then, after the code is working well in real life, you start thinking about how to make it fast and efficient at a larger scale, for *millions* of users.

That kind of thinking is almost a universal thing in good software development. It just makes sense. And in UX we should think in a similar way. However...

Computers don't get tired; they always follow instructions and can make millions of decisions per second. Human users, not so much. Humans are lazy, distracted, uninterested, inconsistent, and, frankly, sometimes just a straight-up facepalm (but never blame the user!). So, we can't just copy-paste everything developers do into UX. Just because a design works for *some* users doesn't mean it works for *most* users.

VDP is the UX version of the programmer's goal: make sure every minute you spend on work is spent well.

Value, Diagnostics, and Probability Work Together

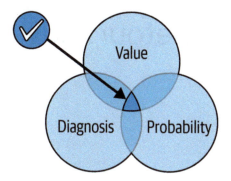

Using these three methods together, UX can "move the needle" for an entire company.

Value is the "make it work" part. It doesn't have to be pretty or perfect or complete; you just need to solve the user's problem in a way that helps the business. Two things, at the same time. Nothing else.

Focus on moments when value is created: the purchase, download, or commitment. Creating new value can launch a new feature, your first cookie recipe, or a whole company from scratch! For the first time, it *works*.

To "make it right" we need *diagnostic* design. Work backward from the critical moment, diagnosing each step from the end to the beginning, making each step easier for the user. A lot of real life UX work is diagnostics, done with data and good old-fashioned research. Or free cookie samples.

A solution that creates value and works well will probably grow! We need to optimize it by considering *probability*.

The more users, the more probability plays a role. Preventing a million users from accidentally deleting a file is a big improvement! 2% more sales for a company selling $50 million is a million dollars more! Probability doesn't make an ecommerce store work and doesn't make the products good, but it can really improve the total sales.

Value is the first priority. It has to work. *Diagnose* problems to make it right. Go from a rough prototype to a reliable product or service. *Probability* improvements can then make your design a fine-tuned value machine that scales well.

Everything in UX can be approached like this. Everything! So, let's look at a whole bunch of examples...

Quick Detour: Advice

Most Advice Is Bad Advice

Before we look at examples of designing things, a note about advice from the internet. There will always be way more people with Level 1 experience than people with a lot of experience. Why? Probability! Everybody with Level 50 experience also has Level 1 experience! Many people get a few levels of experience and then become project managers or professional cuddlers or whatever and never make it to Level 50. Probably because they were guessing, rather than designing, and got discouraged when nothing worked.

My point is...professional cuddling is a viable career move from here! No, wait, that wasn't my point. My point is: most of the people offering UX advice on the internet actually don't know a lot. Ignore them. (Some do! Follow them!) Most are explaining what they *just learned*. Or they believe that UX is just some UI tips and tricks to follow forever. They only believe that because they haven't measured any of those "rules," or haven't seen when they fail.

Before you decide to follow design advice from the internet, ask yourself if you're willing to risk your job on their level of experience, which is probably not much higher than yours.

OK, on with the show!

A Simple Button

A Button Is One of the Simplest Things to Design. Or Is It?

Just a button

I want to begin our design examples with something deceptively simple. That is, it looks simple, but it's not. It's actually extremely dangerous.

We're going to design a button. Starting with no information.

I know. I am nervous too.

For a UI designer, drawing a button takes about a minute: draw a rectangle, choose a color, adjust the corner radius, add a clever label nobody understands, aaaand they're done. Or—they might have a design system! Then they just drag it onto the screen and bam! Done. Then they simply push it around the screen one pixel at a time for a few days, stand back and look at it a few times, stroke their chin, and voilà! They have designed a button. But is it the right button?

(For the record, I am being very cheeky. I design lots of UI buttons myself. It takes *at least* five minutes.)

For a UX designer, wireframing a button is the last 30 seconds of a *lot* of work and research, if you're doing it right. Knowing how to design a button—or if you *should* design a button—means knowing a lot about the user and business, long before either of them need that button.

It's Just a Button. How Hard Can It Be?

| Normal Button | The 6-Month Button™ |

I call it the 6-Month Button™.

The 6-Month Button is a button like any other. It doesn't take longer to draw—a minute or so. It works the same way; users click it. It has a color and a label and all that. It's just a button! But the code behind it is so complex that it will take six months to build.

At work, I often joke that I can create six months of work in 60 seconds, so developers should be nice to me. When I say it, the 6-Month Button is a funny threat, but as the UX designer all you have to do is get reckless once, and the 6-Month Button can appear.

Designing a button with no information is dangerous because we can lead the rest of the team down the wrong path.

Is a Button the Right Answer?

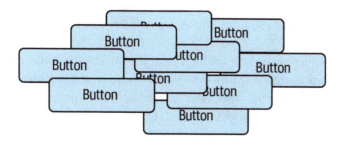

UXers are famous for questioning the question instead of answering directly, so let's try it!

Since you have no information, ask: Is a button the right answer? Why a button? Can we *simplify* something instead? Is this button fixing a mistake that can be prevented? Can we write better copy so people don't need this button? Are we adding to a popular feature with a long life ahead or a zombie feature that might be removed soon (a waste of your time now)?

Younger designers (or lazy ones) often forget that features add up over time. This is just one button, and *you* didn't make all the other crap, but you might design 200 buttons during your time at this company. Have you considered the other 199 that you haven't made yet?

Always *subtract, combine, or undo* whenever you can. More stuff requires more technical maintenance and makes your product more complicated over time. *Reducing* things as you go will make both users and developers happy.

Take a History: What Does This Button Do?

Like the good doctor, we need to learn about our patient, the button. The first, best, question is, What will this button do? And the answer we are looking for is about *value*.

There are three main types of buttons in the world, each with a different relationship to value: constructive buttons, special buttons, and destructive buttons.

A constructive button *adds* value in the business model. In other words, when the user clicks it, value is created, or the user moves closer to creating value.

A special button is *essential* to value. If a business model gets so much value from a button that it is hard to succeed without those clicks, then you might want a special button design.

A destructive button *removes* value in the business model. That might sound like a dumb thing to do, but they are necessary and important buttons.

Let's look at value-driven design principles for each type of button.

Constructive Buttons Add Value

There will be many key clicks or decisions during the users' journey that directly or indirectly help the business model succeed, like registering, inviting users, buying more data, posting new content, etc. Those buttons *add value* to the business model.

Often constructive buttons are just one step on the way to creating value, like the third step in a five-step registration process. It's still a constructive button! If a user just turned their brain off and clicked all the constructive buttons, they should eventually do something valuable for the business or themselves.

When you work through the business model in your company, you should be able to answer a simple question about every constructive button: How does it *help?*

Constructive Buttons Need *Higher* Probability

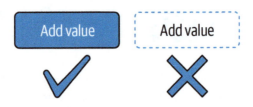

I call these *primary buttons* in *UX for Beginners*, and that is a more common name for constructive buttons, because we *want* users to click them. Therefore, we should design them so they look like you *should* click them!

Constructive buttons should be easy to find, easy to see, and easy to understand when the user needs them.

To make a button easy to see, make it big, use a high-contrast color, make the label clear and action-oriented, and put the button in a good place on the page. Make it look clickable!

If it is something the user could do at any time, like registering, then put the button high up on the page—maybe even in the main menu—so every user has access on every page. Or, if it is something specific, like saving your new email address in the settings, you could put the button directly next to the form where the user types their new email address.

Special Buttons: Constructive Buttons That Are Make-or-Break

Sometimes there is a feature that is so valuable it needs special treatment. Think: Amazon's 1-Click purchase, or Facebook's thumbs-up like button. These are opportunities for a special button.

Amazon's 1-Click button skips almost the whole checkout process, making purchases very easy. The convenience is very high and the conversion rate is very high: excellent value for both user and business. Not a button for users to miss! So they gave it a unique design.

On Facebook, likes aren't just a button for the user who clicks it. Likes give feedback to the user who posted the content, spread the post to the button-clicker's friends, and every like teaches the feed algorithm to be smarter. Facebook doesn't just *want* those clicks. Facebook *needs* those clicks for Facebook to work! But when Facebook was new, likes were also kind of a new idea, so they gave it a unique design.

Give especially valuable clicks a special button design.

Destructive Buttons Reduce Value

Delete	Cancel	Remove	Unsubscribe

Destructive buttons are exactly the opposite of the constructive buttons: they *decrease* value in the business model, like deleting an account, removing users, downgrading to a cheaper subscription, or deleting content that was already posted. Those actions all make the product or service *less valuable—for the business*. But they are still valuable to the user. We need them!

Without destructive buttons, we would have problems with privacy, security, bullying, overspending, unused accounts adding up, and so on. Although these buttons reduce value *in the moment*, they are important for the business in the long term.

It is important to make destructive buttons easy to use, but not *too* easy. (It's a rookie mistake to *hide* destructive buttons from users. Don't do that!) If a user wants to delete their account, so be it. However, we don't want to *encourage* people to destroy value, and we definitely don't want to destroy value *accidentally*.

Destructive Buttons Need *Lower* Probability

How do you make something easy but not obvious? Use probability backward!

There are two common ways to approach these buttons.

In modern UI design, one common solution is called *ghost buttons*: just a border to define the button, and the button is the same color as the background so it *blends in*. In *UX for Beginners*, I call these *secondary buttons*. Subtle buttons lose the battle for attention whenever a primary button is on the same page. Easy to see, hard to *notice*.

However, a very destructive action (like launching a nuke) should feel like a warning, not a whisper. In those cases, a good solution is to design it as a big, red primary button, but place the button where it isn't likely to be clicked accidentally. Usually that means lower down on the page (make the user scroll a bit), right-aligned, away from where the user is focusing their attention normally.

Appropriate Friction

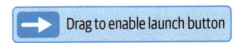

Speaking of nukes: in movies, when the president is being forced to launch missiles at gunpoint, he often needs to press a button, protected by a glass cover, activated by two keys, requiring two codes, used simultaneously, and known only to a few people.

That's not just a terrible movie plot, that's appropriate friction! UX used to *prevent* a button click.

Whether we're talking about money, time, or millions of human lives, some actions—like launching a nuke—are more "expensive" than others. In those cases, we want to add *friction* for the user, so they will only complete the action intentionally (i.e., not by mistake).

Appropriate friction should be created with simple actions, designed to make the user *conscious* of what they are doing. Two clicks where one is on the left side of the screen and one is on the right side of the screen are nearly impossible to do quickly. Something like that can be enough.

Ethical Note

A little goes a long way here. The key word is *appropriate*. This tactic is sometimes abused by unethical designers, like when you are automatically registered for a newsletter and can't find a way to unsubscribe. Or when the "Delete account" button is on a weird screen, 10 clicks away, in a little menu you would never expect. Or when insurance is added to your purchase by default because you didn't deselect it.

We use *appropriate friction* to help users avoid mistakes they will regret. But if you take that too far and *hide* buttons or trick users into doing things they don't want, you will hurt the business in the long term. You might even break the law. There is a big difference between maximizing success for the business and manipulating users to make a little more money.

A Modal

No Button Is an Island

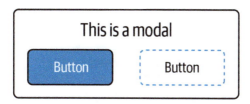

Any real design combines many smaller ingredients (buttons, text, colors, content) into bigger clusters that serve a purpose. The kids call it a *layout*.

For example, our little button might be part of a modal/prompt. (You might call it a pop-up or a lightbox, but I call it a *modal window*, and I am the author, so I win.) When someone says "pop-up," you might think of annoying ads or subscribe-to-my-newsletter requests, but a modal can also be something that forces you to pay attention, like when we need to confirm that the user *really* wants to delete their meticulously curated collection of sneezing panda videos.

In that case our button isn't just a clickable rectangle. It's a decision!

The modal design should be based on the research we have done to understand the business model and work with (or against!) probability to create or protect value. The same ideas of constructive and destructive actions still apply here.

Constructive and Special Modals Need *Higher* Probability

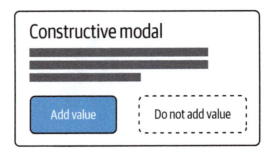

Usually, a *constructive* action is going to add value, and *usually* we don't need to warn the user before they do something valuable. But from time to time, a constructive action is so expensive or hard to undo that we should double-check first. For example, if your software can send an email to a million people or order a new Tesla, a *little* appropriate friction is a good idea.

However, we want that click, so the constructive modal's design should extend the principles of a constructive button.

Align the button and text so the user's eye naturally follows from top to bottom. The text can be short and sweet. Don't assume the user will read everything. If they have seen this modal before, they might skip the reading and click the first big colorful button they see! Make sure that button does what they want—and we want—when they click it, and don't add any other distractions.

Destructive Modals Need *Appropriate Friction*

A destructive modal should feel like a warning. Big. Red. Alarming. Our goal is to make the user pause and consider what they are doing, rather than clicking something by reflex.

We want to help the user *not* click the destructive button by using probability. The destructive button should be quiet, maybe even a link. Position it away from the bottom of the text, usually on the right side (assuming you read left to right). The label can be long—as in "Destroy everything you love forever"—so they read or skip it. And we should add another button that *looks constructive*, but actually just cancels! Why? Because if the user isn't paying attention, they will just cancel. No harm done. They can always try again. If they really want to delete their account, a brief pause to read is all that is required.

Let's make this more interesting, shall we? Let's design a whole page.

A Page

Let's Combine a Few Design Clusters into a Whole Page

 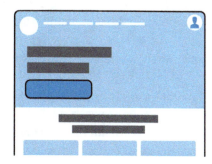

In this book I might say *page* or *screen*. It's all the same idea. A page combines many elements into one space: buttons, headlines, paragraphs, images, tables of data, diagrams, videos, animations, sounds, and your deepest, darkest childhood fears.

The user experiences those elements *together*. They influence each other. Like we saw in the modal example, one button can take attention from another button. That's true for everything, not just buttons.

A page design will also cause the user to experience the elements in a certain *order*. By now, you should understand that order is important for probability. Pages are often vertical in general, because of scrolling, but tables and text are consumed horizontally too. Order is two-dimensional!

Suddenly it all seems a bit overwhelming, no?! Don't worry, just follow VDP like always.

Take a History: What Does This Page Do?

Remember that a business model defines value as user needs and business needs at the same time. When in doubt, start there and think about what you're designing.

Who, what, when, where, why, and how does it *help?*

Who will use this page? What will they do here? What do they *want* to do here? What do they *expect* this page to be? When is this page relevant? When is it not relevant? Where do the users come from to get to this page? Where *should* they come from? Where will they go next? How will they use this page?

Every page should have a specific purpose: *Why* this page? Don't just design a bunch of pages because you think "a thing like this needs pages like that."

Most importantly, what is the *one thing* the users should achieve on this page, if they only do one thing?

Take a History: A Lead Generation Page

A common type of page design is a landing page where the user can request more information about a product or service. Marketers and salespeople call it a *lead* when a user expresses interest like that. The purpose of this page is to generate leads.

The value of a page like this is fairly easy to see. It gives the user a bit of information and a way to start a buying process and allows the business to identify a potential customer.

After taking a history, we might learn that these customers are accountants (who) who need a way to organize customer contracts (what) at the end of the financial year (when), which is a very busy time for accountants! Our software must work together with another popular accounting service (where), because it is required by law (why). The marketing team needs this page to specifically capture leads who are *senior* accountants, who they will target with a campaign in the next few months.

Take a History: Pricing Page

Another common type of page is a pricing page where a customer can choose the subscription that is right for them. Something like this: "For 50 dollars you get a high five, and for 100 dollars you get a high five and an ice cream; and for enterprise pricing, please contact sales."

The value of this page is actually quite critical. This is the page that begins a self-service purchase! The user will decide which price/features seem to satisfy their needs, and for the business, obviously, it's a money thing.

After taking a history we might learn that the customers are professional sports bettors (who) that need a way to optimize all of their statistical research (what) during the football season (when). The users are mostly based in Europe (where), and it's harder to make a really good betting income without carefully managing your bets (why).

You Know Too Much

Normally the UX team should think as if they are the user, but just for a moment, let's assume that "we" is the business, not the users. Because what *we* understand is different from what *they* understand.

As the designer of a page, we understand everything about it. We know that our lead generation page includes a "Get the free brochure" button halfway down the page. We know that we make more money if the user picks the annual subscription instead of the monthly subscription. We know what happens when you click the button labeled Share even though we can't see those options. We know that the big image on top is our newest product. And so on.

Users don't understand these things until they see them.

Designers are not superior people; we just have superior information about our own designs.

Prioritize the Clicks You Prefer

On any page, all clicks are not created equal. Usually there are one or two clicks that are very valuable, and the rest are just nice to have. That's important for how we diagnose problems and use probability.

If you would prefer that they click button A, put that at the top and make it obvious. If you show them button B first, they might click that instead! We might know that the best button is halfway down the page, but if they don't scroll that far, they won't click that button because they haven't seen it. That's our fault! That being said, don't *hide* the options that make you less money if the users want them. Just prioritize the clicks you prefer.

The first rule of designing layouts and interactions is to remember what the user knows and doesn't know *at any moment*. You might expect the wrong behavior because *you know too much!*

Scrolling Is Navigation

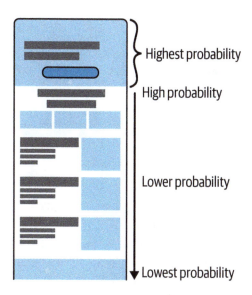

Unless you do something creative or create a link to a spot halfway down the page, users will experience the top of the page first. If the user wants to see more than the top of the page, they have to scroll. Therefore, scrolling moves the user to another part of your design they couldn't see yet, therefore *scrolling is navigation.*

Most users will scroll, at least a little. *But!* Not so fast with your infinite pages there, buddy....

Remember probability: users must go through the top to get to the bottom. Therefore, *the longer the page, the fewer people will scroll to the bottom!* It's not unreasonable to think of the lower part of your design as if it is one click away, even though you don't need clicks to get there.

The top of your design is a *default*. Since everyone starts there, the closer an element is to the top, the higher the probability it will be seen.

Protip: Looking Versus Seeing

Looking   Seeing

Looking at something and *seeing* something are not the same thing. It's the difference between subconscious and conscious thinking.

You might *look at* someone's T-shirt without *seeing* the hilarious joke on it (note: often, young kids see text without reading it). If we assume you know the joke because you looked at the T-shirt, we might be wrong! Some things that you design only need to be looked at, like lines and background colors. Some things you design must be *seen* and *understood*, like button labels and errors, if you want users to *act* on that information.

It Is Hard to Stop Scrolling!

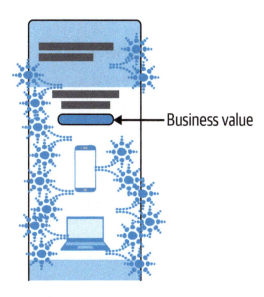

Business value

Talented visual designers (as opposed to those of us who make ugly wireframes all day) can fall into a trap: creating a page design that is so cool and beautiful that it makes you want to *keep* scrolling all the way to the bottom, past the button where the company makes money! Oops.

In UX you might hear someone talk about *scroll inertia*. Inertia (in-ur-sha) is the idea that it takes more energy to stop than to keep going. Apple.com is full of special effects and amazing photos that make you want to *explore* the page, rather than read it. But if you copy Apple on your own page, where the goal is to get more registrations, you're in trouble. What you might not have noticed is that the pages designed to sell and convert don't have any of those fancy visual things. More efficiency, less entertainment. And completely intentional.

If you want users to stop scrolling halfway down the page, don't keep entertaining them beyond that point.

Visual Hierarchy

> # Your eyes go here first
> ## Then probably here next
> Then you may or may not read this content
> Then you may or may not read this content
> Then you may or may not read this content

Every designer learns about visual hierarchy, or how to make a page *scannable*. But not as many can explain why, without using the word *scannable*.

The general idea of a visual hierarchy is pretty straightforward: you make important stuff bigger and darker and less important stuff smaller and less powerful in the layout. Headlines get priority, while required legal links in the footer can be smaller.

From a cognitive perspective, that means users don't have to spread their attention across the whole page at the same time. Users can focus on each piece, just for a moment, and understand them one at a time.

In other words, it's just less work for the user's brain to look at a page like that. They see it in *chunks* instead of one big mess of content. And although that is enough reason to use the principle of visual hierarchy in your designs, we're also interested in how it can help the business side too!

Use Visual Hierarchy to Control *Probability*

> # Best selling point
> ## And the highest probability headline
> Details about the selling point above
> Details about the selling point above
> Details about the selling point above
>
> # Second selling point
> ## Was the second thing you read
> Details about the selling point above
> Details about the selling point above
> Details about the selling point above
>
> # Third selling point
> ## Made you skip the small text above
> Details about the selling point above
> Details about the selling point above
> Details about the selling point above

Your brain treats bigger, bolder things like they are *closer* and smaller, lighter things like they are *farther away*. And your brain wants to handle vision *in that order*. We can use that!

Specifically, we can use it to increase the probability of the user seeing the *right stuff*.

First, make visual *groups* of related stuff and give each one a big, high-contrast "entry point." For example, on our lead generation page, make a list of selling points with a headline like "Why you need this." On the pricing page, give each package a big title and then list all the features underneath.

Then, *order* those little content groups on the page, so the most valuable stuff will be scanned first. The user should scan our selling points and then see the registration form, in that order, because they won't register if they don't understand *why*.

We also want to present the subscription pricing in the right order, but that requires a little more thinking for us...

Design Good Comparisons

Choosing a subscription is more than looking or seeing; it is a decision. And we also want to help the user make good decisions—for their own value and for the business.

Humans make most decisions by *comparing* things. We use the information that is in front of us right now, we compare what we see, and if we feel good about one of those choices, we choose it. And that's how we should design any page where a choice happens.

First, remove anything not needed to make the choice. It's just noise to the user. But include everything you want them to consider while they are making this choice! Remember, they will only compare what they see.

We already know the user will see the choices in the *order* we show them. But also consider how the order affects the user's perception of the choices. If you show the cheapest price first, the more expensive price will look *more* expensive. If you show the expensive one first, the cheaper one will look *even cheaper*. A "free" choice is often a good thing, but it should feel like it isn't quite enough for most users if you ever want to make money.

It is valuable to control which information the user sees, and in which order they will see it, so the most attractive choice for the user is also the most valuable choice for the business.

Google *decoy effect* if this interests you: by adding a terrible choice that is similar to, but obviously worse than a more expensive option, you can actually persuade more people to choose the expensive option, because it looks so much better *by comparison*.

Be Ethical When You're Designing Choices

Never *force* a choice. It's not as clever as it might look.

When customers feel like they get a lot for the money—even when they pay a lot—they are more loyal. Happy customers will actively promote your company to their friends and followers, renew their contracts every year, and even *upgrade* over time as they use your service more and more. Unhappy customers will definitely tell their friends and followers, but not in a good way.

Always *motivate* a choice. Help users *understand* the choice in a persuasive way but *tell the truth* and *let them choose*. If a customer only needs the cheapest subscription, that is exactly what they should buy. Your job is to make products and services that are so good a customer will want *more* over time.

It's more ethical, but it also won't kill your company—usually a plus.

A Flow

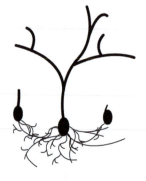

One Type of Information Architecture: A Flow

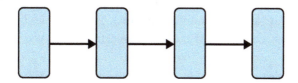

Now that you can design a page for a purpose, let's link a few pages together to make a *flow*! Most of the pages you ever design will be organized as a *flow* or a *structure* (which we will learn about in the section "A Structure").

If you have signed up for anything on the internet, you have experienced a flow. It often includes forms. The buttons at the end of each step probably say Continue or Next. A flow usually creates or destroys something like a purchase, or an account, or posts a video of you lighting yourself on fire in the shower.

What really defines a flow is that you always do the steps *in the same order*. A flow can be easily diagrammed using a *flow chart* that illustrates the main steps or decisions that are made during a flow.

But before we get into all that, let's talk about *conversion*.

Conversion

A word you will hear a lot in UX. *Conversion* is the percentage of people that complete a flow (or any start-to-finish process). For example, if 100 people put something in their cart and 3 of those people actually pay, your *checkout conversion rate* is 3%.

This whole idea of probability applies to conversion too. 100% of the users *started* the flow, but only 3% *finished* the flow, and if you measure how many people are still in the flow after each step, you will see that it gets less and less along the way. Why? The same reason more people see the first menu item than the last item: everybody who does the third step also did the first step!

There are a lot of reasons why people might drop out during the flow: form usability, confusing errors, the length of the flow (measured in time), the difficulty of the steps (measured in swear words), and even just lack of motivation! We can control some of those problems, but not everything.

To improve conversion (i.e., get more people to finish your flow), think about everything you request from the user like a *cost*. Every question is a cost. Every minute is a cost. Required questions cost a little more than optional questions. Confusing questions cost even more. If they have to go get their credit card or upload a document, that is a big cost. Negative surprises like a big shipping price is a huge cost.

Then, just design the flow that does everything you need, at the smallest cost for the user. Trust me, if you attack a redesign project with "user costs" in your head, you will do well.

Especially if you understand the purpose of your flow first.

Take a History: What Is the Purpose of This Flow?

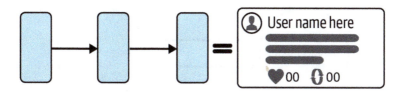

In *UX for Beginners*, I introduced the idea of "content objects," which are the key *things* that your designs are dealing with. On a social network the content objects might be posts, users, and groups. In HubSpot, it might be contacts, companies, and campaigns. In Spotify, it's songs, artists, albums, and playlists.

More often than not, a *flow* creates or manages a content object. A user is created when they complete the registration. A company is created when a user fills in the company's details. A group is created when you give it a name, description, and invite someone. Those are flows.

The reason we use flows to create content objects is because they are *predictable*. We know exactly what is needed to create a user, group, or company, every time. And as a UX designer you will actually spend a lot of time gathering requirements for content objects or flows and understanding why those requirements are needed.

But we can also influence those requirements, and we should!

Design Is a Two-Way Conversation

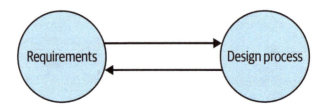

"Gathering requirements" might sound like flow design is a one-way process: gather requirements, then make the flow that fits those requirements. That's not wrong, but it's not the whole story either.

An ecommerce checkout requires certain information to execute the payment and ship the product to the customer, for example. Those are real requirements. We need them to make it work. But do we really need the customer's gender, age, and phone number? The marketing department might think so but remember: each question reduces sales. If nothing breaks without them, they are *soft* requirements, worth discussing.

And often you should compromise! If a phone number allows you to decrease fraud, it *is* worth a small drop in sales. That's a good *trade-off*. The best UXers are masters of managing trade-offs.

The point is: your job is not to gather wishes and make them come true. Your job is to create the most value possible for users *and* the business.

Requirements will define the flow; the flow will define the requirements.

A Flow Includes *Time*

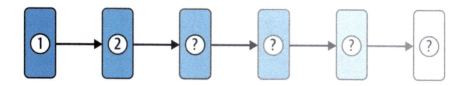

Until now, we have been focusing on individual pages, happening all at once(ish). A flow is the first time we have looked *across time*: several pages that are experienced in a sequence, but not all at the same time. You can still scroll those pages, and each page has many elements that affect each other, but now we must consider how the user will *anticipate* future pages and how their recent experience will affect what they are doing now.

Diagnosing problems includes *when* symptoms happen! And again, what does the user know *at this moment?*

If the shipping costs can't be calculated until step 2 of your form, then you should tell customers that. Or, if you know how much shipping will cost, tell them up front. You'll save the user from anticipating the extra cost, and they won't be angry when the final price isn't the price they saw at the beginning! That is the effect of *time* on your flow experience. Things *change* in the middle!

Similarly, if the flow is long, and especially if it is difficult, you should communicate the user's progress. Show them how many steps are left, where they are now, and make their progress visual by "checking off" the steps they have completed. Make it easy to go back and make changes without losing everything they have done. Nothing will make someone quit a flow faster than feeling like they screwed up and it is ruined!

Before you design the individual pages of a flow, step back and be diagnostic about the flow itself, as one big design. Fewer steps, easier steps, less mistakes, more flexibility, and better communication with the user along the way.

Be successful by making users successful.

Design Each Flow for What It Does

Every time I see a UX designer jump on Dribbble to get "inspiration" for something really functional, like a flow, I roll my eyes. A good flow is not a matter of trendy layouts and cute icons; it is 98% about making it smooth, easy, and efficient. When you have that working well, you can add whatever "delight" you want. Preferably at the end, after the user converts.

To design a good flow, you must consider all the requirements and risks (!) that it contains. On the following pages I'll give you a bunch of examples of requirements that should change the design of your flow.

OPTIONAL OR REQUIRED?

One classic conversion consideration in form design (whether it is one page or several pages) is whether you actually *need* the user to answer every question. As a general principle, try not to ask questions if you don't need the answer. It is really common to squeeze in questions like "Where did you hear about us?" or "What is your hat size?" just because somebody wants to know. If those questions are not technically *required* to finish the flow—nothing breaks if the user doesn't answer or if they lie—they are *optional* questions.

Probability says we should get as much *required* information before asking anything optional and *help* users skip the optional things they don't want to answer. That might be a little counterintuitive. Why would we *help* users *not* answer a question? Because it is *way* more valuable to get a new registered user without that optional answer than to lose the whole conversion because they felt uncomfortable sharing their hat size in the form.

GET THE VALUABLE STUFF FIRST!

Optional and required form input is about getting information we *need*. But even within the required questions, some information is more *valuable*. A common example is the user's email address. If you have a two-step registration and the user quits after seeing the second step, it would be nice to still have their email address so you can email them.

Sometimes that type of decision causes a cascade of other choices. For example, if you want the email address, you might need the user to approve the terms of service too, so that becomes another requirement in the first step. If you want to use their name in the verification email, maybe you need to collect that in the first step too. However, since their password isn't required until *after* they verify their email address, maybe you don't need that yet. When you really think through every piece of a design, half of it just falls out of the requirements.

HOW FAMILIAR ARE THE QUESTIONS?

Some flows are everywhere. If a flow is made of questions like name, email, password, password again, phone number, address, and information like that, your users have seen it all before, even if they are old and not super technical. Forms were paper first! Familiar questions can be combined into longer steps, and all as one column; and the labels on your form inputs can be shorter and simpler, because users already know what to do. You can say "Email" instead of "Type your email address." There is nothing wrong with the long version, but it's the long version! Unless your flow/form is unconventional somehow, just let users get through it quickly.

But if it *is* unconventional, like measurements for a suit or questions about your criminal record, then let the user slow down. Make the labels more informative, provide help text to explain if needed, and use fewer questions in each step so users can take a breath once in a while.

SPEED OR ACCURACY?

The faster users can get through your flow, the higher the risk of errors. The slower they finish, the more accurate their input will be. The question you should ask is, Which of those is more important? The answer might even be different from question to question.

If a user can edit the input later, like their name, then maybe it's OK to risk a typo here and there so the user can finish *faster*. It doesn't break anything. But if it will cause a problem, like a typo in your password, then you should *minimize errors*.

Group all the *speed* questions together and all the *accuracy* questions together if you can. When you want speed, be ruthless and reduce the "user costs" to a minimum, even if it causes very little mistakes. But if a typo will hurt the experience, make the labels longer, give help text, and help users slow down a little.

INFORMATION OR CONVERSIONS?

One of the most common trade-offs is related to how much information you want to collect during the flow. When you collect leads from that amazing landing page in the previous section, it can be very valuable to know the potential customer's company name. It allows salespeople to look them up before sending an email to follow up. But *requiring* a company name means all the leads who are just curious for personal reasons will hesitate or quit or enter something that screws up your customer relationship management system (CRM). Fewer questions means more conversions. But more questions means you can do smarter things—or even use automation—with every conversion. If you don't *want* personal conversions (higher *quality* leads), just require the company name!

Be diagnostic about this one and spend time with your colleagues and customers to understand how each piece of information could be used. Weigh the value of both.

HOW NECESSARY OR VALUABLE IS IT, FOR THE USER?

There are situations where the user *must* complete the flow: digital tax returns, university applications, or the paperwork to create a new company. It can be simpler than that, but in those cases "conversion" is much less of a problem because the alternative for the user is not filing their taxes, not applying to university, or not creating a company. The cost of *not converting is too high to quit*!

In real life, unfortunately, these are often the worst forms in the universe, because the owners don't care about conversion rates. Everybody converts! But if you get to design a form that is required for something important, I beg you: show users that they are making progress, help them avoid mistakes, give them a chance to prepare documents before they actually need them, and let them save their progress.

EASIER STEPS OR FEWER STEPS?

This is a classic debate, and it will happen to you. Is it better to have more, but easier steps? Or less, but harder (or longer) steps? There isn't a right answer, and you have to A/B test each case to know for sure, but there are a few general guidelines that might help:

1. Are there natural groups of questions, like a bunch of questions about your job or family? If so, group those questions together so they make more sense and the user feels a sense of completion after that step.

2. Are there any steps that are not forms? If a user just needs to make a choice like "Pickup or delivery?" or "How would you like to pay?" or "Choose a file" or "Take a selfie," then it can be nice to isolate that as one step. It feels quick to make one easy choice at a time if there aren't too many of them.

3. Are there any choices that determine what the user will do next? Something like choosing pickup or delivery changes which page the user will see next, so you might be *forced* to isolate that step. That's OK! See it as an opportunity to do something *really* nice and easy.

4. Put the hardest steps—essays or cover letters or uploading documents—near the end and tell users they are almost finished. One exception: if users must do something creative in a flow, like creating an avatar, they might be more likely to complete the flow *after* their creation has been made. Otherwise, they lose all of that hard work!

HOW OFTEN WILL THE USER DO THIS FLOW?

A registration flow is a one-time thing. Each user only needs it once. But some flows, like adding a new contact or creating a task or making a blog post, are things a user will do over and over.

In one way, this is a risk, because it means every little bit of friction in that flow will be experienced many times. So, spend time smoothing out the details!

However, if you know users will do it again, you can capture information the first time that makes the experience better the second time. For example, when you share a Google doc with someone, Google can autocomplete email addresses of people you know. This is the motivation behind tools that save your password or autocomplete common forms as well: the less work it is, the more a user will do it. Usability increases probability!

ARE YOU JUST GETTING INPUT, OR ARE USERS MAKING CHOICES?

Forms are where my mind goes when I think of flows, but that is not always what a flow is made of. *Choices* are also a type of input. Do you want your pizza delivered, or will you pick it up? Do you want to rent a car or an SUV? Which project will this task belong to? Would you like a window or aisle seat?

These types of choices are not just text input, and sometimes they make the flow *branch*. If someone wants the pizza delivered, they need to enter a delivery address, but if they want to pick it up, they choose a pickup location. One flow can go in two directions. If you want to rent an SUV, that might filter the list of vehicles on the next page so the user doesn't have to look through a long list of irrelevant Ferraris (annoying!) If you assign a new task to a project, you can offer the user a way to assign the task to people working on that project.

This means the flow is changing in real time, without leaving the page the user is on, which is great, but it also means you need to consider all the ways those choices can be combined...are there scenarios where the user doesn't know what to choose? Are all of those choices required? What happens if they choose a project with no people assigned to it? The more sophisticated the flow is, the longer it takes to build and the harder it is to design, but sometimes the best design solutions require the designers and developers to do more work so users can do less.

IS IT LONG?

Sometimes there is no way to avoid a super long flow. It might be a complex form, or it might be something important like a college application having a lot of information, documents, or decisions (like which dorm you want to live in, whether you want a meal plan, or whether you plan to steal another school's potbellied pig mascot as a prank [usually optional]). When the flow starts to feel like a lot of work for the user, it's good to chunk it into sections or steps. But how do you decide which questions, input, choices, and actions should be grouped into each chunk? Think diagnostically!

Look for questions that form a reasonable topic. All the questions about your preferred roommate might go together. All the questions about your area of study and books might go together. Payment-related details like your address and credit card info can go together.

It *feels* easier to do related things at the same time, because it keeps your brain in one place.

ARE THERE LEGAL, FINANCIAL, OR SECURITY RISKS?

Some requirements are just standard legal requirements, and as long as you include them, you're fine. For example, you must get consent to send someone newsletters (you can't autocheck the box for them). They might have to agree to your terms and conditions too. You might want a phone number for two-factor authentication. And you'll need to confirm an email address or phone number many times during your UX career. Those are some common ones. All good so far.

But if your flow has serious legal, financial, or security requirements, slow down! Design carefully. Banks often require *contracts* or *antifraud* questions to become a customer. Large payments are catastrophic if done incorrectly. Data breaches cost millions of dollars, and identity theft is everywhere. Super easy and convenient flows can also make it super easy and convenient for criminals!

Sometimes a little appropriate friction can prevent *a lot* of problems.

How Should We Measure a Flow?

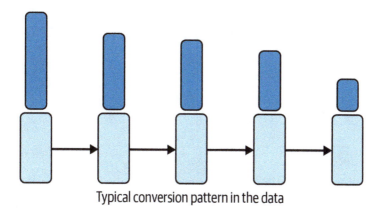

Typical conversion pattern in the data

A simple enough question. If you want to diagnose problems in your designs (or redesigns), you will have to measure your flow.

Since a flow is a predictable sequence of steps, the best way to measure it is to count the clicks on the buttons that take the user from one step to the next. Then you should compare those numbers in order so you know how many of the people clicked the first button, the second button, and so on, all the way to the big valuable button at the end.

The difference between the first button clicks and the second button clicks tells you how many users dropped off in between. If any one step seems like it is losing a higher percentage of users than the rest, that is your first symptom. Keep going to diagnose the problem in that area of the flow!

When you design a new version of a step, you can measure the new version against the old version with an A/B test. But actually, it is important to understand why different versions of a design should exist, so let's talk about that next...

Quick Detour: Redesign

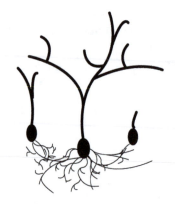

Design Is Redesign

I have mentioned a few times already that you should make a design, measure it, learn something, and then use that new information to design it *again*. When you design the same thing again and again, improving it each time, that is called an *iterative* process. You are *iterating* on your design until it gets really good.

That is the *only* way to be a good designer.

Some people think that means you have to use an agile process, but they are not the same. A good design process doesn't need to follow any particular project management method, but you must revisit your designs over time.

Even more than that, if your design will be used in more than one context, such as desktop and mobile devices, you should actually have more than one version of your design *working* at the same time!

Reasons to Design More Than One Version of the Same Thing

There are a million little reasons to design versions of something in real life, but a few of those reasons happen more often:

- *Different devices:* Different screen sizes or input methods (tap, click, etc.) are the most common reasons to design more versions of something. A big layout for a laptop with a cursor just doesn't work well on a small phone screen with a finger. Not to mention tablets, televisions, AR, VR, etc.

- *Different users:* If you have beginners and professionals using your app, it might be a good idea to hide advanced stuff by default and reveal more functionality if needed. That's called *progressive disclosure.* That's not the only way you can accommodate different user profiles, but it's one way.

- *Different content:* Especially with data-heavy products and services, it is likely that you will have to design something where the content is less predictable. For example, if some users will post 10 times per year and some users will post 1,000 times per year, it is unlikely that one layout will do both in a good way.

- *Change over time:* Just because your design was amazing two years ago doesn't mean it still works. As the world changes around your designs, you should come back to them and see if they still work, or if your work since then has changed the requirements.

- *A/B testing:* If you want to test a new hypothesis to see if it performs better than the existing design, you need two designs at the same time so you can compare. Sometimes it is the *only* way to know which one is better.

Should Everything Be Responsive?

One of the classic "perfect world" things you might have learned at a boot camp or in a book is the idea that your designs should work well on every imaginable screen size. Well...yes and no.

"Mobile first" is a smart approach to design where you design the mobile (i.e., smallest) version first to make sure you don't overload the design on a small screen. It is much easier to *add* features on a big screen than to *remove* features on a small screen.

But in real life, not everything needs a mobile version. Not all mobile versions should try to do what the big version can do. Google's Sheets app is a stripped-down spreadsheet viewer, with very little functionality. Google Sheets for desktop is a powerhouse tool that does so much you'd need a whole book to show what it does.

So, the short answer is no: everything doesn't have to be responsive. Consider what is *needed*, and design that.

Consistency Isn't Always a Good Thing (Functional Inconsistency)

In general, consistency is a good thing. As long as it's part of the same context, stick to a small number of styles: a few button styles, a couple of fonts, one main menu, one or two submenus, one link color, and so on. The less users have to learn, the faster they will learn it.

But some people take consistency too far. When the context changes, the design *should be inconsistent*!

A common example is mobile platforms. Apple iOS and Android are different contexts. Different hardware, user habits, design guidelines, and app stores. Therefore, it is completely reasonable to have slightly different designs for those apps. Unless your users will sit with two different phones in their hands and use both versions of your app at the same time, you won't gain much by forcing both app designs to be identical.

Functional inconsistency: it works better *because* it's inconsistent.

But there is one exception worth pointing out.

Brand Isn't UX

UX can definitely make the experience of a brand better, and they should definitely work well together. But UX and brand are different animals. When a UI designer wants to change the logo and colors to match every trend that comes along, it becomes clear that they don't understand branding.

A good brand strategy defines principles for how the company talks, acts, and looks *everywhere*. Although it should be a little flexible, brand strategy is *universal*. There are literally rules to follow! UI designers should be especially sensitive to branding conventions because more consistent brands do better over time.

If an iOS user switches to Android and downloads your other app, the functionality and UX can be a little different, but that user should instantly recognize it as *your app*. Because the *brand* is the same, even when the UX isn't.

Branding should be *consistent* across contexts. UX can be *inconsistent* when it makes sense. Everybody with torches and pitchforks can find me on X: @joelmarsh.

A/B Testing Is Science, Not Guessing

Diagnostic design is about looking for evidence, forming a hypothesis based on that evidence, and then *testing to verify your hypothesis*. An A/B test is when you split the users between your new design(s) and your old design, and measure to see which design gets the most clicks, conversions, likes, goats, or whatever.

An A/B test is *proof* that the new design works better—if you do the test well. Here are the rules:

Rule 1: Don't talk about the A/B test club. Or do. Whichever works better.

Rule 2: Focus on subjective hypotheses. When your hypothesis is more emotional or cultural or just based on user preferences, it can be hard to measure objectively or clearly. That makes A/B testing your best friend.

Rule 3: Wait for statistical significance. If you stop the A/B test before you reach the necessary number of users (software can say when), you haven't learned anything. It doesn't matter which version looked like it was going to win.

Rule 4: No guessing! If you are doing diagnostic design properly, more than half of your A/B tests should be positive results, and it shouldn't be weird to see 10% or 20% improvements. Guessing gives you a bunch of "1% better" results.

Rule 5: Keep it simple! (But test many versions if you want.) Stick to one hypothesis or one design change or maybe a whole new design. If you want to test five different headlines, do it! But remember that you will need enough users for each version! Complicated A/B test results are hard to interpret, so why bother?

Rule 6: Be efficient! Do plenty of research. Wait for a good hypothesis. But when you have one, definitely test it.

Rule 7: One test at a time! Two A/B tests can affect each other. But when you know something works, keep it (until you think of something better).

A Structure

Another Type of Information Architecture: Structure

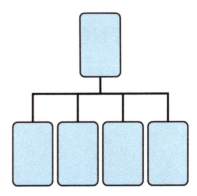

I mentioned before that most pages you design will use one of two types of information architecture: *flows* and *structures.*

Flows are predictable because we can design exactly the sequence of events we want the users to experience. But when we design the *structure* of a website—many pages connected by menus and links—we can *influence* what users will do, but we can't control it completely.

Structure determines how users can move through your designs. The more effort it takes to get from page A to page B, the fewer people *will* go from page A to page B; so again, we're back to the idea of probability. But structure is also one of the most powerful tools in UX to improve how well your designs *work.*

Build Structure Around Value, Not Semantics

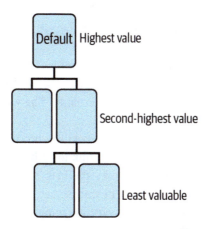

I have seen some extremely complicated methods to research and design page structures, but the idea of value is the most effective approach I have found in real life. And when we talk about structure, we often mean *menus*.

Many UXers make the mistake of trying to design *logical* menus. Like "animals grouped by natural habitat" or "types of clothing from head to toe" or "departments in our company."

All terrible. All common. But it's not obvious *why* they are terrible.

On the surface, it might seem ridiculous for me to say that your menus shouldn't be logical, but *logic* doesn't make your menus more *valuable* in the business model. A dictionary is extremely logical, but is it the best book you have read? No. Is your favorite book amazing because it is well organized? No. Same for menus.

Nobody chooses Coke or Pepsi because one is more logical than the other. We don't go to a clothing store thinking, "I need to cover my torso with something," so organizing clothing by body part doesn't make sense *to the user*. We think about shirts and pants and jackets, indoor and outdoor, seasons, and social expectations about what to wear (i.e., men, women, etc.). So those things make sense to users in the menu, even if they don't share a logical rationale.

Organizing your website based on the org chart of your company is surprisingly common...and literally couldn't be more unknown to a customer if you tried. Nothing says "we don't think about our customers" more than designing the customer-facing website according to non-customer-facing information.

Probability Should Define the Structure

Your general approach to structure should be: create the shortest paths from the default page (usually the home page, but not always!) to the highest-value pages or content you have.

It's not a coincidence that the default screen in TikTok (and Instagram and Facebook and X...) is the feed. *Content, engagement,* and *advertising* all happen right there, and engagement drives the advertising! The vast majority of value in those apps is created on that screen.

And from high-value pages like that, repeat the process again: What are the most relevant, highest-value pages you can link to with the *next* click? and so on. That creates a structure of links that gives the user the most valuable possible, as soon as possible. The deepest pages in your structure (i.e., the pages that take the most clicks to find) should be the lowest value, or the least frequently needed pages, from the user's perspective.

Don't Stop Yet! Leaving Is Still an Option.

When you have determined the general structure, the second phase of information architecture (IA) thinking is how your users or "traffic" will *move through* the design. When linked together, your pages become *paths*, and the ideal structure will keep users moving, instead of forcing them to stop or go backward.

Will they be stuck after they click down to a deeper page? What will they need next? Do users need to visit several sections to do a task? Are they working through a list of questions? If they go back, do they lose their place on the previous page?

If you don't give users somewhere to go, they might leave. It is shocking how many designers forget to consider *leaving* as an option when designing navigation.

In user analytics, the *exit rate* is the percentage of users that leave from each page. Users will always leave your site eventually, but try to make sure they are leaving because they are happy, not confused.

Analytics: Diagnose Structures as a System

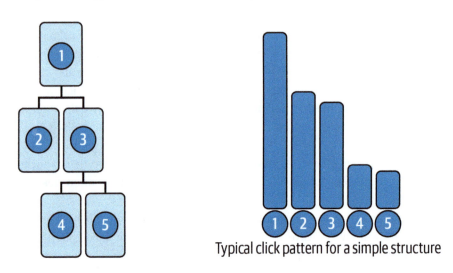

Typical click pattern for a simple structure

When doctors listen to your heart and lungs, they are thinking about them as part of a big system, not just individual body parts. The same is true for pages in a structure; they're a system!

Earlier, we learned that data makes behavior *visible*. When you look at your analytics data, we're not looking at each individual number; it's a system! We're looking at *patterns*.

I once diagnosed a problem with *copywriting* because the data and the structure showed different symptoms. Out of six identical pages, users spent much longer on one of them and converted from that page much more often. The cause? A different person had written the copy, and it was much better! We had them rewrite the other five pages, and it worked.

As we have discussed, probability should create predictable patterns in your data. When something in the data doesn't *fit* the pattern or seems kind of extreme, it's worth looking at it a little more.

Speaking of which, let's look at a couple of structures.

A Three-Screen Banking App

Real banking apps can be complex, but as our first example of structures, let's imagine a bank account app with three screens: one account, transaction details, and settings.

On the home screen the user can see their account and pick a transaction (money in or money out) to see a few details. Easy-peasy.

For simplicity, let's say this app is just used to double-check transactions, once or twice per year. Definitely an *efficiency* problem (not entertainment). And something this basic is a "hygiene" app—we need to have it, but neither the business nor the customers really *want* to use it. So, clean and simple is the plan.

This structure creates what I call *in-and-out* navigation, which is often easiest to build. You go *into* a transaction and back *out* to the account. That's it!

We Also Need Settings

As simple as our banking app is, one reason it might be useful could be the settings. A little place to keep your contact information up-to-date, or answer KYC (Know Your Customer) questions for antifraud reasons.

The value of those settings is *even lower* than the account and transaction information, since we only need it every few years; but it's important when we need it, so it can't be hard to find. Let's say we link to it from the main account page, but we put it up in the top corner away from the transactions.

Now we have a three-page structure where the user navigates in and out between two of them most often and uses the other one, settings, when needed.

If we make a *site map* of this banking app, we should draw it in a way that helps the viewer see the relationships between the pages, if that is useful.

Diagnosis: This Is an Efficiency App

Let's say we check the analytics for this app every few months, and it usually looks the same: users visit once or twice per year, they view one or two transactions per visit, and the average visit is about 10 minutes long. On the surface, this might sound like a pretty boring app, but I see a problem in those symptoms. Do you?

It is a really common mistake to think *engagement* is always a good thing. If this app created *entertainment* type value, it would be. But this app is about *efficiency*.

Does *10 minutes* for *one or two transactions* sound efficient to you? Sounds pretty long to me. I'd bet you a dollar that user interviews will reveal a long, slow, tedious process of hunting transactions in a long list, just to find the one that users want.

Time to gather some symptoms (if they exist!). Who uses this app? Which transactions are they looking for? Do those transactions have anything in common? When did those transactions happen?

Probability: Make It More Efficient

Although this is hypothetical, I would guess the most recent and biggest transactions will be checked more often (probability). Let's assume the data and users agree, and we have a hypothesis! How can we improve the design?

First, certain transaction details are more relevant than others: the date and amount are what users mention most. Let's show those directly in the list so they are easier to find.

We could also "lift" the most recent large transactions automatically. Either with some quick filters for the user or by showing them at the top of the list by default. No need to search at all!

We have just analyzed the data pattern for an *efficiency* app, found where it differed from what we *expected* in theory, gathered symptoms to find a common cause, and designed a solution for that hypothesis! VDP.

If we see a different data pattern when we launch the new design (2 minutes per transaction instead of 10 minutes), then we can feel good about our diagnosis.

Another Structure: A Three-Page Portfolio Site

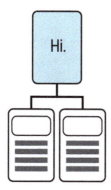

Let's say you're designing yourself a portfolio website, and since you're new to UX, you only have two cases (but good ones!). So, you make a home page and two pages for your projects. In-and-out navigation like our banking app.

But first, what is the *value* of your portfolio?

To you, the value might simply be showing what you have done, or you might want to use this portfolio for job applications, or to be discovered online for Elon Musk's next hostile takeover. That's why I made mine!

For the users, including Elon, the value of your portfolio would be the other side of those things. Maybe they are trying to hire a good designer or looking for a designer with your type of experience. Either way, a portfolio is a content site, rather than straight facts and data like our banking app, so we have a few more things to consider.

Is a Portfolio Efficiency or Entertainment?

A portfolio *doesn't* fit nicely into my two big, dumb types of value—efficiency and entertainment.

You do want people to quickly see what you have done, and the amazingness of your projects should be clear and easy to understand, which sounds like efficiency. But it's also *content*. It should be interesting, cool, impressive. And you want your users to read and see every detail of everything you have made. That sounds like entertainment.

It might be both!

A portfolio *should* be entertaining to look through. If you are a UX analyst, maybe a little less so. If you are a UI designer, a little more so.

But it should also be efficient. As much as we *want* every user to read everything, you should design it so they *don't have to*. That might seem counter-intuitive until you think of the *user* value. Recruiters have a lot of portfolios to look through, so the *less effort* it takes to see your value, the higher the *probability* they will.

Diagnosis: Users Only See One Project?!

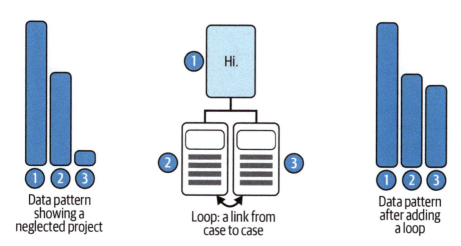

Data pattern
showing a
neglected project

Loop: a link from
case to case

Data pattern
after adding
a loop

A month or so after launching your portfolio site, when the paparazzi finally leave you alone, you decide to check your analytics. You are horrified to see that most users only see *one* project, and it's usually the same one! One of your projects is barely ever viewed?! Why, God, why?!

Let's diagnose it.

Earlier we said that your structure design should consider where users will go *next*. You forgot that part, because I made it sound like in-and-out navigation was a good thing now too. But the context changed, so the same solution might be wrong!

Your projects are long and require engagement from the user. Transactions are short and are only for quick information. That's not the same at all! So, if we don't want users to leave after viewing the first project, maybe we should link directly to the other project at the end.

As you can see in this example, that one link turns your site map into a loop. It's not in and out. It's round and round!

Probability: Why Only That Project?

By now, you might be able to guess: the *first* project on your portfolio's home page will get the most clicks if all things are equal. It's the first one users see. Two years from now, when you naively change your LinkedIn profile to Super Senior All-Knowing UX Designer, that list might be long, and the projects at the top will be even more popular than the ones at the bottom, statistically.

But probability can surprise you too. If someone famous tweets about the ninth project in your list, it will be exposed to way more people. More people = higher probability. It will stand out like a firecracker in your data.

Or, if the first project is called "Highly Precise Measurements of Paint Drying" and the third project is called "Launching My Neighbor's Car with a Homemade Trebuchet," your data might reflect the subtle difference in *entertainment value.*

In reality, factors like these combine to make life interesting. We just need to figure it out.

Why Does a Loop Work?

The link we added to create a loop will help users who loved your Trebuchet project continue on to see what else you have done. They might be surprised how awesome drying paint can be!

The reason it works is because users want to keep moving *forward*. When they can't, you force them to pause and make a conscious decision about what to do next. So, when they do that, put a good click in front of them! Remember, they have scrolled all the way down the page to read your first highly entertaining project. If you could load the second project directly on the same page, that would be even better, but if you can't, give them more projects to choose from.

A structure where every project links to a bunch of other projects creates a never-ending set of paths around your site, so users will continue *forward* more often, until they are fully satisfied and contact you for an interview.

Little Loops Become Big at Scale

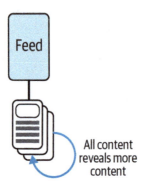

All content reveals more content

Loop structures are more powerful than they might look. When you put 100 million people into a loop structure and you make money with ads on each page, suddenly you are multiplying *all the money your company makes*! If that loop increases the average user behavior by just one more page, it might earn *billions* of dollars in ad revenue!

Many common social apps, like Pinterest and Instagram, use loops. Every post is followed by an endless list of *related posts*. When you tap one of them, you get *more* related posts. Next thing you know you're 100 taps deep in makeup tutorials and an hour of your life is gone.

If that was simply an in-and-out structure like the bank transactions, you would navigate into one post, then back. Then into another post, and back. It makes you think too much, it makes you go backward, it reveals less content (and less *targeted* content), and you would lose interest much sooner.

A Simple Business

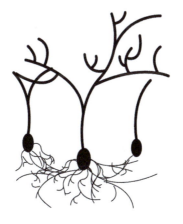

Let's Start with an Ecommerce Site

OK! Now we're talking. A design with an actual business model.

An ecommerce site can be huge (like Amazon) or small (like stores selling baby clothes on Shopify), but from a UX perspective they are all rather similar. They create value by offering a bunch of products (user value), which users find via categories (in the menu) or by searching. When users find something they like, they put it in their cart or bag by clicking a button to save the product. After saving things they want, the user goes through a checkout flow, which ends with a purchase (business value).

Notice that an ecommerce site has both a *structure* when looking for products and a *flow* when the user is paying. Interesting! This mixture of information architectures means we have stepped up a level in complexity, and because of that, we will see more complex behavior in our data.

Different sites will sell different things and require different designs but fundamentally create value in the same way.

Understand the Brand!

One of the defining characteristics of ecommerce is that the marketing and brand matter *a lot*.

One of the reasons all ecommerce sites are similar is that users are not using it because they like the *store*. Usually, successful ecommerce sites are successful because of the brand, or the unique products, or because they have become trendy in general. Therefore, the UX people must have a deep understanding of what *motivates* the users to want the products or love the brand.

The UX of the website itself is *pure efficiency*. Your job is to get them to the products they want as smoothly and easily as possible, and then make the purchase obvious and painless. But the UX of the products might have some entertainment value, depending on what the products are.

Ecommerce UX should motivate, support the brand, and otherwise *get out of the way*!

Value 1: Browsing and Finding Products

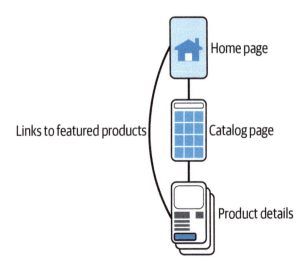

Let's talk about the user behavior in the *structure* first.

One type of shopping behavior is browsing. It can be driven by curiosity or a dream of owning something they can't afford or just keeping up with trends, but browsing has no specific goal. Users wander around, influenced a lot by how the structure helps them (or not), looking at anything interesting.

Finding a known product, either through text search or specific clicks, is very *intentional*. Finding a product requires the user to know what they want, or at least the *kind* of thing they want, and often they have researched it before. When you see eye tracking of this behavior, it is clear that users are trying to *match* the idea of what they want with the images and menus they see, ignoring almost everything else.

The structure you design should allow both types of *nonlinear* navigation. Help browsers go *across* sections of the site and help hunters go *deeper*.

Value 2: Buying Products

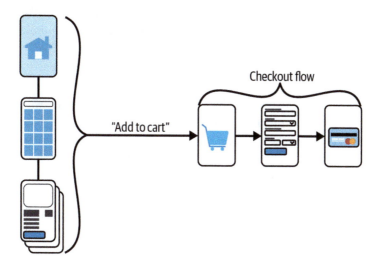

Checkout flow

"Add to cart"

Users can't decide to buy before they have enough information. Ecommerce stores often forget that and put Buy buttons everywhere. Build emotional motivation in the first pages of the structure; add information as the user navigates deeper.

When the user clicks the "Add to cart" button, your UX work shifts gears. At that point we will leave the *structure* and enter the *checkout flow*.

Platforms like Shopify and Klarna are making checkouts more and more standardized—which helps users understand them—but you'd be surprised how persuasive a good brand can be. The more customers want to buy, the more they *will* buy.

Most people drop out in the first few steps; they might not have planned to buy in the first place. But as users get deeper in the checkout, it becomes more and more painful to lose them. They were so close! Work backward from the last step in the checkout to find and diagnose the most valuable problems.

Aim for Perfection

In UX, there is usually a point where more optimization isn't worth the effort. But ecommerce is a bit special in that way. It makes sense to optimize the hell out of it!

Ecommerce is a common *design pattern* and a common *business model*. But it's more than that.

The value is mostly created by the brand and the products, while the UX should try to *protect* as much of that value as possible (i.e., reduce *friction*). Users are already interested when they arrive on our site; our job is to keep them!

When you work on ecommerce, aim for perfection. A/B test like there is no tomorrow. Since the pattern is so established, you're trying to make it perfect. Every photo, every detail, every click. Talk to customers a lot, consider what expectations the brand is creating, and optimize everything for maximum effect.

Be Quantitative *and* Qualitative

There is no type of business where you will focus on conversion more than in ecommerce. Your conversion rate and average order value will dominate most conversations with people working on the site. Optimizing conversion for ecommerce is very quantitative work. You should measure a lot, test a lot, and dig in your analytics a lot.

However, branding is not a quantitative thing. It's very subjective. And a lot of the numbers you see in your data are motivated more by *entertainment value* than efficiency. That means you should talk to users!

Successful ecommerce brands are invariably run by people who care a lot about their customers, talk to them often, and aggressively try to understand what those customers think and feel. Sometimes a good photo of the fabric texture, a smart sizing guide, or a small technical detail about a product is exactly what they needed to seal the deal. And sometimes the only way you will know that is to ask.

Think About More Than One Visit

It is tempting, when designing something like a store, to feel that you need to *make* users buy right here, right now, or you will lose them forever. But in real life, that's often not actually how people make decisions.

Your ecommerce site should be designed for a few different scenarios, and only one of them is "ready to buy, and planning to buy, right now." You should also help customers who are looking for something *like* what you sell, but they haven't decided yet (i.e., *help them decide*). Make it easy to compare and save things they like so when they come back the second time, ready to buy, they can find it easily.

You should also design ways to *browse.* If someone has just discovered your products for the first time and they are curious, give them ways to look around and see what you have. *Forcing them* to buy doesn't work. *Persuade them* to buy instead.

Then the marketing folks should use retargeting ads to bring them back. ;)

Think in Comparisons

Remember when we said people make decisions by comparing things? Here's a chance to use that principle.

First, understand the *essential details* customers think about when deciding on *these products*. We don't choose dresses and dishwashers and video game consoles in the same way, but each of those things has details that make or break the decision. It might be the fabric or the energy rating or the games that are available for that console (which isn't the product itself at all!)

This is why user research is so critical in the beginning. When you understand the essential *value* customers need to see and compare, design those comparisons. Show close-ups of the fabric, display the energy ratings clearly, or show the top compatible games. No guessing! Do your research!

Oh, and spend a lot of time looking at other sites that sell similar things too. Unless you are the only place to buy these products, customers will compare you to those sites too.

Again: in ecommerce, aim for *perfection*. Details matter.

Use Probability to Sell More

There are lots of places to improve probability on an ecommerce site. Use all of them if you can.

The first big place to use probability is advertising. You can't sell anything to people who can't find you, and it's hard to sell to the *wrong* people. Almost every time a company runs a large online ad campaign, the conversion rate drops, because they get *more* visitors, but the *quality of the visitors goes down*. Think about the probability of your audience being interested before you spend your money!

The second big probability category is "death by a thousand cuts." On an ecommerce site, each little problem might seem small, but enough small problems become a big problem. From the words in your search ads to the thank-you email after a purchase, *optimize the details throughout the whole experience*.

Start optimizing on the last step of the checkout. Losing someone there is worse than losing someone on the start page, so you have the most to gain *as a percentage* by optimizing the end first.

Content-Heavy Products and Services

Content Is the Purpose

Hundreds of articles, questions, discussions, etc.

Let's upgrade from ecommerce sites, which often have some content for marketing purposes, to a site where *content is the purpose*.

Wikipedia is a content-heavy website, and if we were just learning about information architecture and the UX of content in general, it would be an interesting case. However, Wikipedia is also a nonprofit, funded significantly by donations (I have donated for many years, and so should you!), so it's not the best "business" example.

Journalism, on the other hand, creates deep websites with years or decades of archived articles and high volumes of new content published every day, week, and year. A site like that often relies on banners and sponsored content to pay the bills, and the more content users see, the more ads they see, and the more money the site makes.

Let's look at how value is created in a business like that.

Revenue Without Conversion

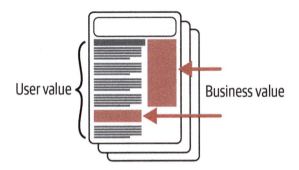

There are two sides to a content-oriented business that makes money through ads: the users who consume the content and the advertisers that pay for it to exist.

For the users, the *value is the content*. They read articles or watch videos because they like the articles or the videos, and that content is free for the users (or users pay to subscribe, but let's keep it simple for now).

For the advertisers, the *value is the users*. More specifically: the value is being *seen* by the users, as many times as possible, or being *clicked* by users to drive visitors to the advertisers' websites.

What you should notice immediately is that *users don't convert* to make money. What?! Users aren't the buyers, which makes it trickier to solve user needs and business needs at the same time.

But if users aren't the ones buying, what do we do with users to increase value for the business?

Page Views as a Priority

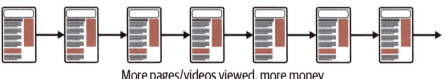

More pages/videos viewed, more money

On a big content site that makes money with ads, the focus of the UX designer is on *views*. Page views (if it is text content) or video views, for example.

Every time a user loads a new page or video, more ads are shown, and the site can make more money. High-quality content should be the first strategy, which is why algorithms try to recommend the best content you might like. However, that's a big (and valuable) technical project, so what can we do with design?

We can make it convenient to find the next article (like our portfolio "loop" structure) or more automatic to see the next video; we can use shorter content to load a few more pages or longer articles to load more ads as they scroll. Unfortunately, clickbait (headlines that tease us into clicking) also works, although you'll probably go to hell for that one. We can also use advertising targeted to the topic of the article to get more clicks, because more *relevant* ads get more clicks.

Time-per-Visit as a Priority

On YouTube, they are interested in views. However, if you were working there, it might be best to *measure* the potential value of those views to the business. Not all views are created equal.

If a user watches one video that is 10 minutes long and another video that is 10 seconds—two views—it can be more useful to think about that as 10:10 of *viewing time*. Multiplied by millions of users, the number of views starts to be a pretty rough measurement, but the *time spent watching* starts to be a really valuable metric for engagement.

Video ads can't take up too much of the time a user spends watching; otherwise it gets annoying. Remember, leaving is always an option. *When* the ads are shown also matters. Users might tolerate a couple ads at the beginning—if they know what they are waiting to see—but at the end? Not a chance.

Thoughtful ad placement can have a huge effect on value.

Diagnosis: Balancing User Value and Business Value

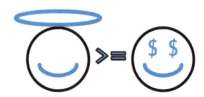

At this point, you might have noticed a potential conflict, or at least asked the question, How many ads is too many?

If more page views and more time watching creates more money, why not pack the whole site full of ads everywhere? Well, because that experience would be terrible for the user, obviously. In fact, some users will even pay to remove ads completely, although it tends to be a weak business model in reality.

Users don't get any value from ads, so the *balance* of ads to content doesn't only have to make money for the business; it also must maintain enough content value for the users.

If you see a long, slow trend of users viewing fewer and fewer pages/videos, you could investigate this value balance with A/B tests. You might have over-designed the advertising, lowering engagement. Long-term, that will kill the advertising business too. Don't be too greedy!

Conflict: User Value Versus Business Value

When business value is prioritized over user value

This is the first example where our users and buyers are not the same people, and we should recognize that, at some point, the business might be tempted to *abuse* the users to make more money.

Like Facebook.

In the early days, Facebook only optimized the feed to sell more ads, so as they collected more and more data, they filled the feed with more and more money-oriented posts. All the while, making it worse and worse for users.

After many years and two billion users had joined, Facebook had created powerful incentives for marketers to abuse the algorithm, and the people seeing the content, and had tied their global business model to those abusive incentives. They were stuck.

Once users started to feel Facebook deteriorating, the brand trust went into the toilet. As I wrote this book, Facebook's stock price, marketing, and the documentary *The Social Dilemma* reflected that lack of trust. I am literally suggesting that the entire issue can be traced back to a conflict between user value and business value.

Another Conflict: Paywalls Versus Ads

In this book, business models are how we create value, but a company can make money in more than one way at the same time! Sometimes, one way to make money can even affect another way to make money.

For example, a journalism site with ads in the articles could also have a "paywall"; that is, visitors must *subscribe* to read some or all of the articles.

Probabilistic thinking will tell you that more people read free articles than paid articles, because everybody willing to pay would also read for free. And the higher the price, the fewer people are willing to pay, usually.

But! What if you don't make enough money on subscriptions to make up for the ads you lose because less people are reading? Or what if you can make *more* money from subscriptions than ads, *even though* you have less readers? Or, maybe you should mix some free ad-driven content with some paid subscriber-driven content?

Hmm...tricky! No easy answers there; both can work, and data is a very important part of that strategy.

As UXers, we need to be aware of the value for users and the business on any given page, at any given moment. If we design for *page views* because we're thinking about ads but the articles are being viewed by paying subscribers, we might be "ruining" the experience for the most valuable users. If we design for subscribers and we need to show ads, we might reduce the potential of the business. Dangerous for such a delicately balanced business model!

It would be *correct* to design two "flavors" of this UX: one optimized for more views (ads) and one optimized for conversion and reading experience (subscribers).

Observe Long-Term Trends

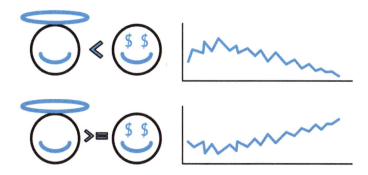

UX people often look at data for the last 30 days. Once in a while, you should look for insights in data from a longer period of time.

When I get access to analytics for a new site or product, I usually start by setting the date range to *all time*, and then I click around to see how the data looks. Not only does that give me a sense of the trajectory of the product in general—is it going well?—it also allows me to ignore large one-time events, like that time The Rock said our app was his favorite guilty pleasure.

Another great reason to do that is because we're usually doing *short-term* work. All those little changes can *accumulate* into a big effect, and we will only know this if we look at bigger data.

For example, the trend of page-views-per-visit could be slowly going down over a year, and we might ignore that because each design change increases the number of *advertising clicks* we're getting.

An easy, but very common mistake.

Probability: Your Best Content and Users

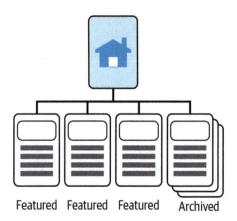

Featured   Featured   Featured   Archived

When you have a lot of content, there are some great ways to use probability that benefit everybody.

The more content you have, the harder it is to find the best stuff, and that is nobody's fault. That is a good motivation for features like "newest articles" or "popular posts." Especially on the start page, those easy features allow new users or casual visitors to quickly see the best your site has to offer. Better content is the fastest way to a user's heart, and profit.

You can also ask, What is the best content *for this user*? New users need to get something good without much effort, but regular visitors might need the most recent articles within an area they have visited before. Personalizing for experienced users and recommending the articles that usually trigger the most additional clicks can be powerful with a lot of users.

Another good optimization is smarter navigation, but that is a whole subject of its own...

A More Complicated Structure

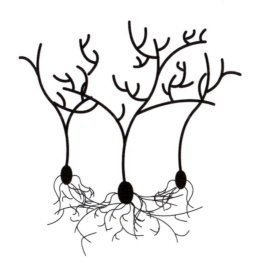

Most Real Products and Services Are Not Simple

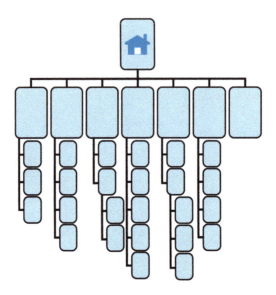

In the interest of being a good teacher, I started this book with the fundamental principles of value, diagnosis, and probability, and then proceeded to show some simple, but realistic, examples of how those things can be applied. And I suppose I have been throwing in some tips and tricks along the way.

But enough of that. Let's talk about some examples that are a little more complicated.

Real-life work usually isn't made of basic three-screen apps, and ecommerce is only one of many, many, types of businesses—one of the more predictable ones!—so it really wouldn't be fair to let you think that's how your real work will look.

As the complexity of your product or service grows, you should be more careful. Each design choice you make becomes more powerful! Not just more powerful in a good way though; also, in a destructive way.

When a Site Is Big, Structure Is Very Important

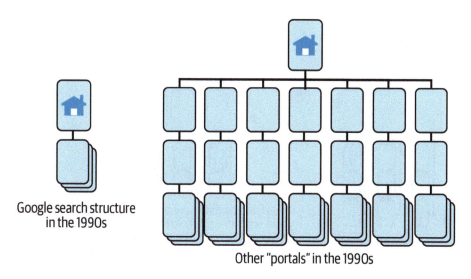

Google search structure
in the 1990s

Other "portals" in the 1990s

Structure is very important *anyway*, but the bigger it gets, the messier it will get unless you are actively managing your designs. From time to time, you need to take the "helicopter view" and consider where all the small changes are going!

When I say "big" here I mean how many pages or parts your business/design includes. For now, let's just imagine a huge version of the things we have discussed already: a *really* big content website with thousands of articles, a *huge* ecommerce store like Amazon, or even just a complicated assortment of products like Staples or Walmart have.

If we simply do *more* of the things that worked for simpler businesses, we will eventually have a design that takes all day to navigate or is like a maze of menus and decisions that no user will survive. Actually, that's how Google beat other portal sites in the beginning: while others made lists of sites in categories, Google made one list that ranked all websites based on your search. At a large scale, the solution that worked on a smaller internet was just inferior UX.

This is when your design is not as focused on the *value* stuff anymore but is *heavily* focused on diagnosis and probability.

What Should Be in the Main Menu?

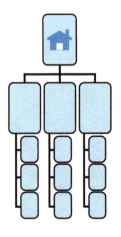

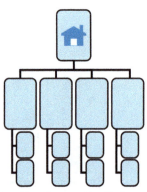

These two structures have an identical number of pages. One needs more clicks to reach the bottom but has a simpler main menu. The other needs less clicks but has a larger menu. Both can be smart solutions.

There are a couple different schools of thought around this sort of thing, especially with older people who do information architecture, but fundamentally, most of that conversation goes back to my earlier point about *logical* or *semantic* ways of organizing a menu: they are all basically equal and not so great from the user's perspective.

Less experienced designers are often surprised that a more complicated structure doesn't necessarily need a more complicated menu (if you're just looking at it, visually). But it can also be surprising that users don't always think a big menu (with lots of options) is more difficult either! It depends!

If you build your structures, and therefore your menus, around the *value* from a user's perspective, then both approaches can work. Users don't care how many times they click: one click that 26% of users understand and six clicks that 80% of users understand are *the same probability of reaching the target page!*

The real question is, How are you managing *information density?*

Information Density

Information density is how much information the user needs to think about at any moment.

It can be helpful to think about *eliminating* options for the user every time they click, kind of like the game 20 questions. In that game, you need to ask smart yes/no questions to guess what object the other person is thinking about. You should ask stuff like "Is it alive?" because any answer will eliminate a lot of options. If your first question is something stupid like "Is it underwear with hearts on it?" And the answer is no, you aren't closer to guessing the right answer.

In the same way, you want each level of your navigation to get the user *much closer* to what they need. Even a site with a *million* pages can be quickly navigated if the menu is designed like that.

Also, the more *emotional* the value is at the time, the lower your information density should be (usually). Apple uses big, beautiful images (emotional) because your first choice is basically just, What type of device do you want to see? But if you're picking stocks, for example, you need a lot of financial detail just to understand the quality of a single company. Spreading all of that across many pages or clicks could actually be very frustrating!

Each level of your navigation should be designed for the job. Don't make every menu the same just for consistency. It can even be *helpful* for users if the upper levels of navigation look different than lower levels because it helps with *orientation*. On Wikipedia, for example, navigating a broad category like *psychology* looks different than navigating within an article about a single psychology experiment. And it should!

Put the Business Value Near the User Value

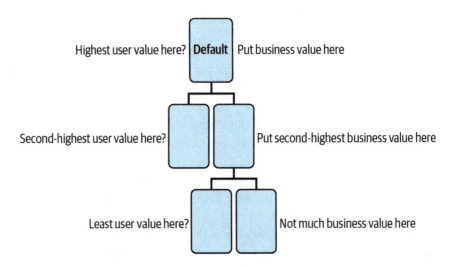

Remember when we learned how your structure should always consider value from the user's perspective first? That means whatever users *value* most is where the navigation should take them, quickly.

And you should *use that* to push the business needs.

By focusing on user needs, you will be able to predict where users will go and where *each type of user* will go and *what those users might be thinking* when they go there. That is a lot of valuable information for the business!

For example, if users come to your website mostly for the discussion forums, it might be tempting to force users to go *through* your ads to get there. Don't do that. Instead, give the users a clear path to the forums, and show them ads *while they are there.*

By creating value for users *first*, you create a place for business needs to be exposed in a good context and over time will create good reasons to drive users to the things they value most. As you should!

Don't Get That Backward!

It is worth repeating the potential mistake I just mentioned earlier: if you try to satisfy business needs first before you "let" users have what they value, it will open the door for a competitor to destroy you, and it will teach your users to hate you.

If we start making our users go through our ads just to get access to the forums, a competitor who doesn't do that will look like a better product, even if it is otherwise identical. If they can get some users to start switching, we're in trouble!

Over time, the new forum will gain popularity; we must add more and more advertising to compensate for fewer and fewer users (i.e., make the problem worse), and eventually the other forum will win. User-first business models are *superior* in the long term!

Opportunities and risks like that often go unnoticed by executives. Without understanding the diagnostics and probabilities of something simple like navigation structure, they will be mystified why users prefer one forum over the other.

Navigate All the Things: Shortcuts Are Powerful

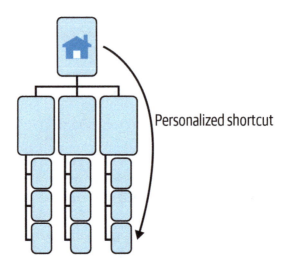

Personalized shortcut

A complicated structure is hard to design, but it can be even harder to change. Technically speaking, once you have committed to a content structure, you might be married to it.

However, you can usually predict that certain *behaviors* will exist, like users having favorite topics or authors, or that they want to see the *newest* content every day. Those are opportunities to let users go *around* your structure.

Intelligent shortcuts that are either controlled by the website ("top posts") or the user's own choices ("authors you follow") can navigate to the deepest, darkest parts of the site with one, personalized click.

The feed in an app like TikTok or Instagram is just one huge list of shortcuts to the best content right now! Think of how many videos you would have to navigate without the feed! Billions?

Start with a general structure for all the things. But instead of redesigning the whole structure as you learn more about your user needs, use *dynamic shortcuts* to reduce the "distance to value" for users.

Search, Menus, Scrolling, Dynamic Content...It's All One Thing

When it comes to navigation, I often compare users moving through a design to people moving through a public place, like Grand Central Station. Menus are like digital signs. Each page is a room. Scrolling is walking from one door to the next.

In the same way, an architect designs the entire subway station as one big series of decisions, so people *move through it*. If every room or sign is designed without considering the rest, you just have a big confusing mess, and people will get lost.

There is a reason we call them information *architects*.

In the same way, you should consider how people will move through your designs, *especially* when they are complex. It's not enough to design each click or page or menu. You must consider every entry and exit point and how a user travels from one step to the next and take the time to reduce the time and effort at every step.

Search as Navigation

Search Is Just a Sophisticated Menu—Or Not

Just now, on the previous page, I included search as navigation. Like scrolling, search is a type of navigation that we often don't *think about* as navigation.

The most important thing to remember is that to use a search well, users need to know what they want. Or the search needs to be smart enough to *interpret* what they want and make suggestions.

In a large, complex structure, search can be an extremely valuable way to find content or access things that would otherwise be hard to find. However, search can also be a wonderful way to get completely lost.

You should intentionally decide what role search will play in the navigation. If it is more of an add-on that will rarely be used, place it away from the main action in your design and make it visually quiet. But if you plan to make your search sophisticated and highly useful, put it in the spotlight!

Just don't switch those. A highly visible and highly useless search is a recipe for confusion.

Google Is the Internet's Main Menu

The most extreme example of search-as-navigation is, of course, Google. You could say that the simplest content structures, like our three-page portfolio site, are so simple that search is unnecessary. Who would waste time searching between two portfolio cases?

On the other end of that spectrum, the most complex imaginable content structure is—drumroll, please—the entire internet. In that case, any "main menu" with a list of items would be so unimaginably hard to understand that we are left with *only search as navigation.*

Similarly, the simpler the structure, the less sophisticated the search must be. Searching among predictable products might be a matter of matching keywords to products. Not so bad. But searching among all human knowledge is, shall we say, a rather different level of ambition.

When you design your search, you should understand the complexity of what users need, what content you are navigating, and how much value search can add (or not) in your particular case.

Bad Search Can Be Worse Than No Search

> **What do monkeys eat?**
>
> What eats monkeys?
> List of albums by The Monkees
> Where are my keys?

In real life, nobody told users that they can only search when they know what they are looking for. It's a fact that actual humans often ignore. Instead, many users try to *guess* what they should search for, hoping to get results that are helpful.

For that reason, if you don't have the resources to create a *good search*, it might actually be better to have *no search*. A bad search on a complex site is like having another main menu along with the real one, except that all the items in main menu #2 (the search) drive you out to the forest and leave you there alone. In other words, they trick users into avoiding the *good* navigation.

Standard menus and pages are usually much simpler (technically) to make and change and measure, so if you can't create a smart search, spend time working on your menu navigation instead. Bring value closer, design good shortcuts, and lift up the best content on the start page.

Then hide the search. ;)

Good Search Can Add a Lot of Value

 I hate my shirt

Most popular shirt style this year

Featured shirts 50% off

Personalized shirt recommendations

On the other hand, if you *can* make a good search, it is an opportunity to drop users onto the exact page they are looking for, or maybe a page full of products or content that are relevant—in one click. That's valuable.

I have seen examples of a smart search *tripling* revenue on a basic ecommerce site. On a big site like Amazon, search is the best version of navigation, so even tiny improvements can add up to a lot of money when multiplied by millions of users.

On large or complicated sites, search is a good investment. If your menus seem to be getting too big to handle, a really good search design project (or team!) can make the site much more *profitable*.

Good search = more money!

On top of all that, search results give you control over what the user sees next after searching, which is a powerful tool. Use it to show them the best content, the most profitable products, etc.

Search Is Hard to Predict: Data Is Your Friend

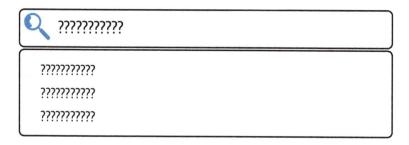

If we are designing a search for a site with thousands or millions of pages (or the whole internet), we are no longer in the world of static design choices. Every part of search is dynamic. We have no idea what users will search for, what results they will see, or whether they will search again.

So, we need to design with *data* instead of *content*.

Large-scale search design is work where you must diagnose problems or find patterns using data. It is also a type of work where probability is your entire view of the world. I know I just said we have no idea what people will search for, but actually, if you have the data, we will know (statistically) what they are *most likely* to search for. Every individual user will be different, but as a crowd, there will be distinct patterns of behavior in the numbers.

Large-scale behavior is too hard to see in individual user tests/interviews. Data allows you to see exactly what the world looks like (statistically). Design the search to match the patterns you see or the patterns you want!

Search Should Have a Purpose

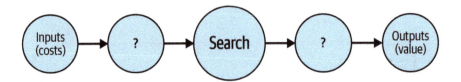

Always start with the business model. What should our search help users do? Are we trying to sell more? Are we trying to build SEO to rank higher in Google? Are we trying to provide education? Are we trying to manage information density?

Another way that search can be like navigation is that we also might fall back on the idea of making it *logically* consistent instead of making it a good way to find *value*. It will be tempting to make your search results into a list of text that contains whatever the user typed, in order of how closely they match...

But that is not how a "good" search is defined! If a user types "jacket" and you are trying to sell clothing, the top result should be the jacket that is most popular or most profitable, even if the word "jacket" isn't in the name of the product.

The *art* of good search design is to deliver results based on what the user *meant*, not necessarily what they *typed*.

Probability: Order Things with Data

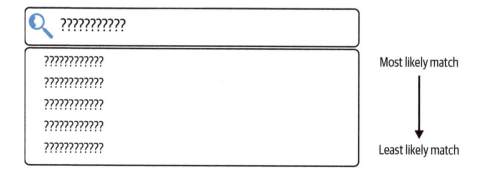

A perfect search would only need to show *one result*. If it is perfect, you don't need more, right? Although real searches are not perfect, the principle is still true: we should optimize which results appear at the top.

At a larger scale, you will have enough data to find patterns and relationships between users and search results. For example, if a user searches for "jackets," there might be 50 different possible search results. If they need support and they search for "I forgot my password," the top result might be an irrelevant issue about forgetting something else. Not helpful!

Use data about *all users* to make the results smarter. If 8 out of 10 people who search for something that includes "password" click the same support article, put that at the top!

You can also sort for business value. If there is no way to know which jacket is a good result, put the newest, most profitable, or most expensive jackets on top. It increases the chance of selling something better!

Marketing-Driven Versus Revenue-Driven Products

Too Much Agency Work Can Warp Your Sense of Value

There are (at least) two subtle flavors of product UX out there in the world, and the designers working on them often don't know the difference unless they have done both: marketing-driven UX and revenue-driven UX.

In the business models we have discussed so far, it is an absolute fact that some of the *value* you can create is value for marketing, and some is value measured in money. But many projects, especially at creative agencies, *only* need to create the marketing part of the value, not the money part. Not directly, at least.

If you have never worked on UX that is measured in money or customers (which is where the money comes from), then you have a blind spot, and my goal over the next few pages is to fix that blind spot.

Brand Value or Business Value?

This headline is going to make some people sit up and say, "Hey wait now, the *brand* is valuable for the business!" And they are absolutely correct. Again, that is why this is a blind spot! If you have never needed to create *business* value—and many designers haven't—then it is easy to imagine that brand value and business value are the same.

They're not.

A product that "only" creates brand value does not have to survive on its own success. It is always *better* if a lot of people use it, if retention is good, or if the usability and value in a brand- or marketing-driven app are strong. But the existence of that product is *paid for* by something else.

A product that creates *business value* makes money. Revenue! If you took away the rest of the company, that product (app, site, whatever) could survive all by itself (more or less). It would sell things or generate subscriptions or motivate certain customers to buy all by itself.

That is a *huge* difference.

The Purposes Are Different

A marketing-driven product is fundamentally about giving your customers or fans *more time with the brand*. This is the rare time when we should separate the idea of an "experience" from the idea of a "product."

If a marketing-driven app, for example, is super fun and makes people love your brand even more, then it has fully and completely achieved its purpose. I once designed award-winning, very popular apps for a vodka company that were used by millions of people. Both apps included some *efficiency* features and some *entertainment* features that were fun at the bar or at a party. Hugely successful, but neither of those apps would last a day if they had to support themselves financially. For the client, they are a *cost*.

On the other hand, every tech startup I have ever worked with has had some kind of software that they sell. If customers aren't willing to pay for it, that's a failure, even if the experience is amazing. That's a revenue-driven product.

The Real Difference Is in the Inputs and Outputs

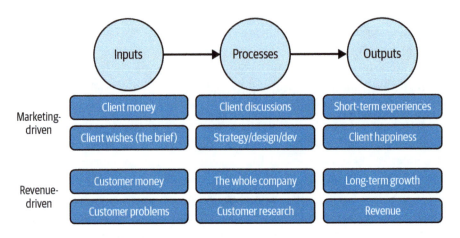

Marketing-driven products are more like big, functional campaigns than products. In the real world, they are measured first by *client happiness*, which has nothing to do with users, and that's how you know you're working on the *brand*. Instead of researching users properly, you will get a *brief*, and the priorities will all be *creative*.

I have heard marketing-UXers refer to "research" as the process of discovering what the clients want! If that is true for you, you are definitely working on a marketing-driven product.

Revenue-driven products *are the business*. They have *customers*, not only *users*. They are measured by things like conversion rates and retention and lifetime value. Those products pay your salary. You will still have stakeholders, but whether they love or hate the product, the customers decide whether it is successful. Therefore, continuous user research is absolutely critical and the business model is fundamentally important.

The *business* is bigger than the *brand* or the "experience." All are types of value but understand the difference!

Quick Detour: Competitive Advantages

Real Competitive Advantages Are Long-Term

If we're talking about the difference between products (or services!) that drive the business, one of the most fundamental differences, compared to marketing-driven products, is how you think about those products *long-term*.

A marketing-driven product is often more ephemeral; you might not intend for it to live or grow forever. Many times, the job of that product is to make a splash in the world, give a lot of people a great, memorable experience with the brand, and if it is dead in a year or two, that's fine. Unsatisfying for people like us who make these things, perhaps, but it's all part of the plan.

A revenue-driven product, on the other hand, should get *stronger* over time, and that will become very relevant as we design more complex products and business models.

If you have ever heard people talk about *network effects*, that is when something has more value when more people use it, like a social network. When two people use it, boring. But the more people who join, the more valuable it becomes. Users can't leave, and competitors can't win.

Lock-in or *switching costs* are similar ideas. Sometimes just using a software tool makes it harder to stop. Like Slack. The free version of Slack was just a way to get companies to start using it. But the more people who use it, the more difficult it is to switch to something else, so a lot of companies just...don't!

Successful companies usually build long-term advantages into their products. You should too. But keep the quality up to avoid customers that *want* to switch; that is a different, but very real, kind of pain.

A Marketplace

Complex Products and Services Are More Than the Sum of Their Features

Buyers   1 + 1 = 3   Sellers

Starting now, we're going to move beyond the "features perspective" on a product. By zooming out a little, we can consider the big, fundamental problems in a variety of different business models.

As our first "simple, but complex" business model, let's look at a marketplace.

Marketplaces, as a concept, are just places where two (or more) groups of people come together because they need each other. The classic case is a marketplace for buyers and sellers, like Airbnb or Tinder or Upwork. In those cases, there are two sides: people offering and renting rooms, looking for "romantic" partners, or offering and hiring freelance services.

The fundamental problem of a marketplace is to get enough people on both sides to find each other. That's it! It's a matchmaking problem! But as easy as that might sound, marketplaces are notoriously difficult to grow.

I will stick to a two-sided marketplace here. The principles are essentially the same if you add more groups but get exponentially more complicated to describe as a design problem.

Supply and Demand as Products

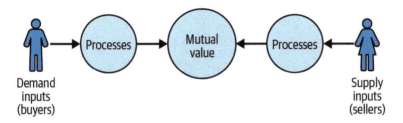

An economist might describe a marketplace as having one side that is the "supply" of something and one side that is the "demand" of that same thing. A buy side and a sell side. Give and take. Top and bottom. You get the idea.

From the perspective of a user, usually only one side will matter at any given time. You might buy and sell things on eBay, but if we look at each thing, you're either the buyer or the seller.

In that way, a marketplace is actually two products! Two user journeys. Two sets of user needs. Two different ideas about what success is.

And those two products need to *meet in the middle*, so there is a very critical *overlap* between the two experiences. Often, that is the transaction where the room gets rented, two people superlike each other, or a freelancer is hired for a project.

Note that the *marketplace* also makes money at the same moment! Two overlapping products fulfilling three needs at the same time?!

head explodes

Marketplaces Make Money in Specific Ways

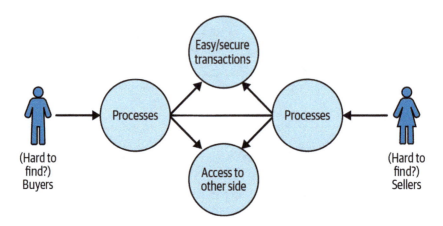

I am sure there are some creative marketplaces out there doing interesting things with money, but generally a marketplace will make money with *transaction fees* or with *membership subscriptions*. And there is a good reason for that.

If your whole business is matching two groups of people with each other, the value for those users happens at the moment when the match is made. By charging a fee for the transaction, the marketplace is solving the *user value* first and then solving business needs in the same motion. It feels *fair*. Nobody would argue that the business deserves money at that moment, when the users have finally found each other.

Depending on what the marketplace does, it might make more sense to charge for *access* to the marketplace and then allow users to match with each other in a more "unlimited" way. If we see Spotify as a marketplace between music makers and music listeners, for example, it would be really annoying to charge a fee for each song. A subscription makes much more sense.

Diagnosis: How Do Users Look for Each Other?

When the two sides can find each other and complete a transaction, it's time to *diagnose* the biggest problems you can find. In a marketplace, the most fundamental value to start with is, How do the two sides *want* to find each other?

On Upwork, buyers usually have a project, and they need a freelancer, like a programmer, to build that project. The freelancers have available time to sell, and they need to find a project that fits their skills.

But *how*, exactly?

User research about the kinds of projects or the knowledge of buyers about what they need or what they consider important would provide valuable clues about the features buyers would find valuable in their search for talent. What if they are looking for all the wrong things?!

But that's only one side of the marketplace!

Research into the needs and expectations of freelancers will also be important. You might need to push freelancers for information that will help buyers find them.

But the real magic comes when you need to find the *overlap* between those two sets of needs.

If buyers want to pay a low price for the best talent and freelancers want to make more money, how can you solve both? If buyers find a good freelancer that isn't available right now, is there a way to still do the deal? How can both sides guarantee that they won't be scammed out of their time and money?

You might make freelancer pricing transparent to buyers, make fees efficient for freelancers, or force payments to happen as the work is delivered. Questions like, How do we indicate the quality of a freelancer? are complicated!

But they are the *right* questions.

Diagnosis: What Percentage of Users Find a Match?

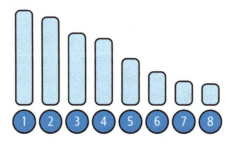

There is probably no "correct" percentage here. It depends on a lot of factors. But as an idea, how *effective* is your marketplace?

As you might expect, if nobody finds a match, your marketplace will die a horrible death. We can use *data* to keep track of how well our marketplace design does its job.

This is another time when you can work backward from transactions to see how many people get to each phase of a match. It's a two-way conversion rate! (Although not as predictable as an ecommerce checkout.) In real life, conversions like this might be called "funnels," but they are basically the same thing.

How many buyers are registered? How many of those post a project? How many of those get attention from freelancers? How many of those get applicants to their project? How many of those pay somebody? How many of those projects are successfully completed?

Put the answers to those questions in a chart, and voila! Start researching where you see the biggest drop.

Diagnosis: What Else Do Users Need to Make a Decision?

The core transaction is always the most important part of a marketplace, but it is not the only thing that matters. If Tinder didn't include images, it wouldn't get very far, even though it is technically possible to find matches without images. People are visual animals.

Similarly, on Upwork, there is nothing *technical* stopping you from choosing a freelancer based only on their profile description. However, to make the decision in real life we need features that help buyers build trust and (importantly) communicate with the people that *look like* a match. That's why Upwork's UI looks more like a search and a chat tool (it's almost a social network, when you think about it!), rather than a purely functional HR tool for recruiting.

On a five-year time scale, most design work happens *around* the core business model, not in it directly, after it *technically* works. Payment options, list-building features, advanced file uploaders, filters, and various user roles are rarely the reason users use a marketplace, but the marketplace might not grow without them.

Cheaters Gonna Cheat

In a marketplace, it is important to realize that users are people, not robots. Although the business is focused on *coordinating* people to find each other, those people are focused on being found, and they don't care about your business needs.

A marketplace creates *competition*. Users want to *win*. That is misaligned with business needs!

On Tinder, it is predictable that many (often male) people will swipe right to like way too many people. Why is that predictable? Probability! If you like *everybody*, then you will match with *anybody* who likes you. Then *you* decide who to choose. You will be *luckier*, in more ways than one.

Upwork freelancers form groups to be seen more often. The real "selling" happens in the chat! In many marketplaces, there is a strong reason to *lie* about quality or experience to fit into better filter categories.

You must consider the motivation to cheat when features are designed. Your designs create *incentives* to behave well or badly.

Probability Kills a Lot of Marketplaces

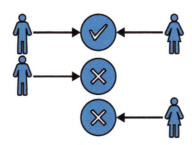

If you are a senior person at any marketplace business, you should obsess over one question: What is the chance of two people who need each other being on this platform, at the same time, and actually finding each other? Your whole business depends on the answer.

Certain types of marketplaces come and go often because probability makes it very difficult to succeed. Marketplaces to find local odd jobs or to sell your old stuff are two good examples. The key word there is *local*.

Tinder is two types of people, looking for the same thing. Theoretically, half of users can match with the other half, and frequently! Upwork is a *global* freelancer platform, focused on freelancers who can do their work remotely, and only people looking for that situation use the platform. Millions of potential users and a concentration of matchable buyers and sellers.

On a local platform, the total population of the city is the limiting factor. But even then, the number of people who *need the service* is much, much smaller. These platforms are often diverse, too, so it's not just people who will mow your lawn or replace your sink; it's people who can do 100 different things or sell random objects and furniture, and each buyer only wants one or two at a time.

And they have to physically connect to do the transaction!

That means, at any time, there is actually a very, very small number of people who can *match*, but lots and lots of users who *can't match*. Helping matches find each other is a *very difficult task*. Growing that business (financially) is also very difficult. And each city is like launching the company again, because remember: the matches must find each other physically!

A local Upwork or a Tinder with 50 different genders or even an Airbnb in a single city would probably fail. The probability just doesn't work in the business's direction.

Marketplace Design Should Increase Probability, Radically

To get more freelancers and buyers to match, you can create features like lists of "saved" freelancers, so you can try to hire them again next time, if they were not available this time. Freelancers can follow up with buyers (and they do!) to see if they need anything more in the future.

Tinder allows likes to match over time, not just right here, right now. In a similar way, that increases the probability of a match in general.

No matter how you do it, try to think of every way to make a match *more likely over time*. Ironically, this might cause you to make *less* search filters, for example, because a more specific search will match *fewer* results. Or you could help sellers answer the right questions so they appear in search more often, or *don't* appear when they *aren't relevant*. Or users could pay an ongoing subscription instead of a one-time transaction fee, so you can continuously help them match.

Supply and demand must happen *at the same time*.

Probability Is in the Nature of a Marketplace

I introduced network effects earlier (see "Quick Detour: Competitive Advantages" on page 165), and now we have a chance to use it. Marketplaces *must* be designed to become more valuable as more people use them. If buyers and sellers leave after they are matched, you won't create a network effect, and the probability of matches will stay low.

I have seen marketplaces that try to get "the best" construction teams to match with people who want to renovate their homes. Nice in theory, hard in practice. The best construction teams don't need a platform like that, so they might not join at all, but there is a strong incentive for those teams to *leave* the platform over time after they are fully booked. In the end, the marketplace becomes the opposite of the goal: only the *worst* construction teams are there. Because: no network effects.

User problems that must be solved repeatedly, or frequently, also make better marketplaces. Fast-food delivery, like DoorDash or Uber Eats, is a good marketplace idea because humans eat often. If we only ate once per year, it probably wouldn't work. Something like Airbnb (an infrequent purchase) works because travel is a *big* purchase. The transaction fees are valuable! A few percent of a week-long vacation rental is not trivial money. Making a few percent of one pizza delivery, once per year, wouldn't be much money, but some customers might eat pizza every week! And a lot of people like pizza!

The more places Airbnb can rent, the more renters will join. The more restaurants Uber can deliver from, the more people will like it. And the more users both of those platforms have, the more places and restaurants will need to be there!

For infrequent or inexpensive tasks, or a small target audience, find a way to turn those tasks into something longer (in time) or bigger (in money). Like a subscription. Or a commitment to buy several times or a bigger project or a membership. Otherwise, probability is going to make your life very frustrating.

B2B Software: SaaS, PaaS, Etc.

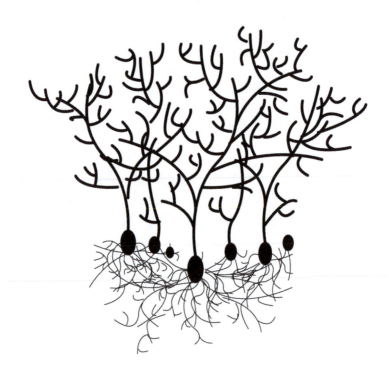

What Is B2B?

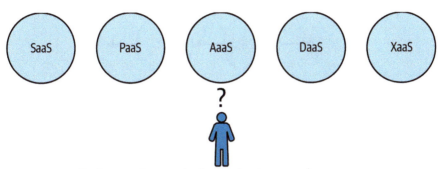

Business customers don't care about your cool acronyms

B2B is simply short for *business-to-business*. (B2C is similarly *business-to-consumer*.) They are just catchy ways of saying who the customer is. And in my experience, that is sometimes the last time the makers of that software think about the customer at all.

There are also a lot of acronyms that end in "aaS" right now. It is short for "as a service," and it is mostly a way for tech guys to feel like they are part of a cool software club. Customers (and half of the staff) often have no idea what those acronyms mean or what the differences are between platform as a service and software as a service and application as a service and data as a service, for example.

Although terminology like that is more of a marketing issue, it is always worth noticing when you're too focused about whether you are technically a "this" or a "that," instead of being focused on what customers actually want, need, and understand. Nobody buys software because it uses a PaaS business model. They buy it because it solves their problems. If you happen to design software that isn't accepted by the Orthodox Church of Software Terminology but it solves the customer's problems well, you will probably be fine.

The important part is this: B2B software solves business problems for businesses.

B2B Versus B2C Versus B2B2C

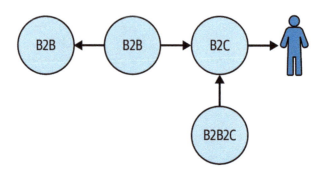

Speaking of terminology, let's clear up a few more words so I can use them without confusion.

A *user* is anyone who *uses* something. Companies (i.e., businesses) aren't real things, so they are never users. If you are tempted to make a joke about "only drug dealers and IT people calling their customers 'users,'" you are old and should get some new jokes.

A *customer* is any buyer, including a business. A kid buying a bottle of Pepsi and a chief operating officer buying supply chain software for a global 100,000-employee shipping company are both customers.

A *consumer* is something else! A consumer is one human being who buys things. Technically, you could argue that you got a sweater for Christmas last year, and although you are "consuming" the sweater and your Aunt Irene was actually the buyer, we don't usually care. Consumers are *all the individuals or households*, not businesses.

> B2B = Customers are businesses. Users work at those businesses.

> B2C = Customers and users are consumers.

> B2B2C = *Your* customers are B2C businesses and users are *their* customers/consumers.

B2B and B2C in General

There are fundamental differences between business and consumers as customers:

- *Quantity and price:* There are *a lot more consumers* than businesses. Something like 30 or 40 people for every company on Earth. If you sell to *big* companies, you might only have a few hundred potential customers, so each sale is really valuable. But if you sell to a billion average consumers, each sale is tiny. But you can have a *billion* of them.

- *Problem depth and cost:* Being thirsty (a consumer problem) is easy to solve, and unless you're dying of thirst, the cost of not solving it is small and temporary. Just get a drink at home! Making your 1,000 developers write code more efficiently, however, is a different story and an *enterprise* business problem. That is expensive to solve, and even more expensive *not to solve.*

- *Marketing and sales:* The biggest difference between B2B and B2C is how we should work with *getting customers.* While B2C businesses often rely on branding and advertising, B2B companies might think of something else when you say "marketing."

Welcome to Sales-Driven UX!

Some B2B software companies offer free or relatively inexpensive software (and I will get to that soon), but right now, let's think about software that is not so cheap or not so simple.

High prices and complex features are *thresholds* for the customer, a barrier that makes it harder to buy. In B2B product design, we should make those barriers as small as we can, but that's only the beginning.

The more complicated the buying decision is, the more customers will need *guidance.* Not just a great website—real help. For that, we need *salespeople,* also known as account managers, business developers, etc. If they are trying to persuade more customers to buy, I mean them.

In a B2B company, when you consider all the ways we can use design to add or increase value in the business model, the customer acquisition process (sales) should be front and center. And unlike B2C companies, the buyers and the users are often different people, which can get complicated.

Buyers Versus Users

Buyers control the money   Users have the real problems

Imagine that your company makes software for HR departments to manage the hiring process. The typical customer decision maker might be the top boss of the HR department: the Senior Executive Vice President of Human Resources and Talent Planning Initiatives (SEVPHRTPI). We obviously need to make this valuable for them; they are the buyer! And anybody with a job title like that must be very important!

But who are the users? Hmmm...wait.

In real life, the SEVPHRTPI might *never* use this software, despite their unquestionable importance. Their decision will be based on procurement requirements, cost, contract structure, and other things like that. The users might be the recruiters three levels down in the HR team or the hiring managers eight to fifteen levels down, who have much less impressive (but distinctly more pronounceable) job titles.

Oh, and the candidates applying for jobs, obviously. Thousands or millions of people. Easy to forget.

In this case, the *buyer* and the *user* are entirely separate people. In reality, you need to please both, and their needs are *completely different*.

What Are You Selling, Really?

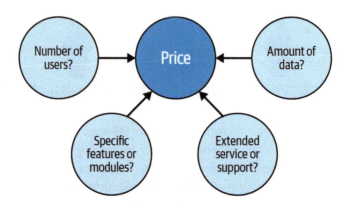

In digital products that solve more complex problems, like HR software, it can be hard to point at one thing as the main value. The "problem" might be the day-to-day operations, which include a lot of smaller problems or tasks. The sales team might talk about efficiency or cost savings or competitive advantages, but what do customers *pay for* exactly?

What we're talking about here is a *revenue model* or a *pricing model*. Literally, what costs what?

In B2B software, we are usually selling something fairly concrete: *seats*, which is the number of users allowed at any time; *data*, like how many social media posts we can analyze each month; *features or modules*, which is the idea that paying more gives you access to more powerful functions in the software; or maybe some combination of those; or something else.

This revenue model has a *huge* impact on the way we design the software itself. Having a mismatch between the pricing model and the software design can *kill the company*.

Design for What You Really Sell

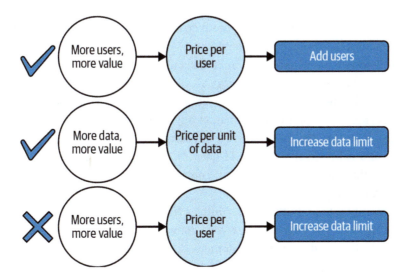

Think back to the example of designing a content site for page views or subscribers. This is a similar idea, but in a different context.

No matter what your product does, customers will get more value from having more of *something*. Ideally, your prices should be based on that!

If HR customers benefit more when their recruiters use the software, maybe you should sell *seats*. Everything in the software should be designed to encourage more *users* (recruiters) to be added. An "Add recruiter" button might even make sense in the main menu! Show how much work each recruiter has already. You can remind admins when an added recruiter has not logged in. You can also limit feature access to registered users, so everybody needs a seat. More users, more value, more revenue!

However, if customers value the number of candidates in the system, maybe you should sell *data*. It should be easy to create and publish more *jobs* instead, because every job attracts more candidates. More candidates, more value, more revenue!

Self-Service Versus Sales

There is one flavor of B2B business models that allows a UX designer (or CX designer, or service designer, or product designer) to be the most powerful salesperson in the company: self-service.

"Self-service" is when a customer can buy and use software without much (or any) contact with a salesperson at all. They register, they pay (usually with a credit card), and they start! This is different from *sales-driven* design because a salesperson is not part of the equation anymore. In a self-service product, we need to make sure the customer can buy easily and that *features* do the selling instead of a salesperson. That "Add user" button is now the way the customer buys, and that gives the product team control over the best sales channel in the company: the product itself.

Remember, though: the more complex the buying decision, the more guidance is needed. The less complex your software is, the better self-service will work for getting (and growing!) customers.

What Does the Company Buy to Make What the Customers Buy?

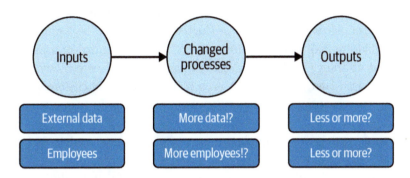

One thing that designers almost always overlook is *costs*. The things that *your* company must buy, including your time, to create and deliver the thing that the customers pay for.

External data, for example. Let's say you're designing B2B analytics software, which collects data from some external sources and displays it for users. If your new design consumes more data than the old design, the cost of providing that service goes up! Adding 5% conversion and 5% cost at the same time means your design created a 0% change overall. Costs matter.

Employees are another example. If your new design creates more tech support cases but adds a highly requested feature, the company might lose money while users give very positive feedback. That's tricky!

Ideally, if you are managing user needs and business needs well, you should recognize these costs and design solutions that *cost less* for the company at the same time they *add value* for the customers.

Revenue Models: *How* Customers Pay Is Make-or-Break

A "revenue model" is the part of the business model that determines how, exactly, a customer will pay for the product/service. It could be a monthly subscription (like Netflix) or a two-year contract (like leasing a car) or a lump sum that is paid up front (like buying clothing at a store) or when you buy "credits" that can be used later. Theoretically, even if the product and customer stay the same, the way the company collects the *revenue* can happen in many different ways!

Revenue models are an important part of all business models, but in the context of B2B software we can really see the effect of choosing one way of paying over another. And choosing the wrong revenue model for your product or service can really change how well the company does over time.

For example, if you sell software for small businesses, your prices might be something like "$10 per month, per user." Makes sense. If you charge that as a monthly subscription, the price to *start using* your software is very small. One user is only $10! But if you require a five-year contract and a minimum of 10 users, then the customer must commit to $6,000 to get started!

Without changing the *price or the customer or the product*, we have changed the way the customer experiences the *cost*. The subscription will be much easier to sell than the contract, even at the same price.

Now let's imagine that customers don't get more value from more users. They get more value from more *data*. That five-year contract is not only harder to sell, but it also locks *you* (the company) into five years of *data costs* and the customer is *unlikely to add more users*.

That mismatch between the revenue model and the product design might kill your company. Or it might not. The difference between those two scenarios is not something you decide...

Impulse Purchase or Highly Considered Budget?

Although the "mismatch" between a product and a revenue model is an objective thing, whether that hurts your business or fits your business also depends on the customer.

Let's keep going with the same "$10 per month, per user" example. Let's also imagine that this is business-critical software, like software for managing a small company's finances. Even though the customers are small and $10 is easier to buy than $6,000, the *decision* about which software to choose is *huge* for the customer. The financial software they choose will change how they manage their money, and the buyer is probably the CEO or CFO. They are going to make this decision *carefully*.

In that case, the difference between $10 and $6,000 is actually irrelevant for sales because they will take the time to talk to a salesperson, and they might still buy an account for all 10 people in the finance department because sharing an account doesn't make sense.

Therefore, self-service also doesn't make sense because everything about the sales process will be contract-based, and therefore it won't change quickly or often. A free trial will work *much better*!

However, if this is software like Slack, for example, which an individual team might just try out of curiosity, the scenario is reversed. A $6,000, five-year contract will kill most potential sales, and a free trial won't give users the chance to grow out of it and add users.

Slack usually begins as an "impulse" buy for a few users because it is so cheap and easy. A monthly subscription and a free tier make more sense to get customers in. When Slack sells to large enterprises that have a long, formal buying process, the revenue model looks more like a long contract.

Protip: Design Around Credit Card Limits

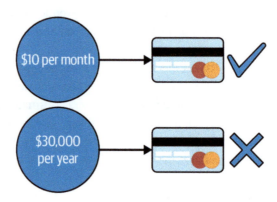

Sometimes, the effort required to make a purchase isn't your fault, but it is your problem.

In many companies, managers and senior employees get a *company card*, a credit card that spends money from the company account but has an individual spending limit. For example, you might be limited to $5,000 maximum for one purchase. (It depends on the company, but often looks something like that.)

If you sell to companies and you sell something that an individual manager can control (like Slack), make sure the total purchase price is lower than the company card limits!

If a price of $4,999 fits under the company card limit and a price of $5,001 doesn't, that $2 difference will radically affect how successful your product is: $5,001 makes the purchase *much harder* because it requires a formal buying process *inside the customer's company*. More effort, lower probability!

You didn't make the problem, but you can solve it. *Design* your prices to work with practical limitations.

Social Networks and
Communities

Users Are the Product

Customers are there for the users

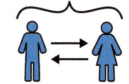

Users are there for each other

You might have heard the phrase, "If you're not paying for a product, the product is you." That phrase is often applied to social media, where users are getting everything for free and advertisers are paying to be seen on the same platform. Our attention is the product, from a business perspective.

While this is true, it is a cynical view of social networks as a platform we can design. We often forget that a social platform must be fun in itself before there is anything to sell to advertisers. The product we sell is not the product that users use. So, what *is* the product that users use?

That's an interesting question, actually. If there are no users on a social network, what is its value?

In fact, the value for users is *also other users*! That isn't just true because of money; it is true because of what a social network is.

Human Connection as a Feature

It is easy to think a feature is something we see or click in an interface. But that's not quite right. A feature is just a *method* of getting something to happen. The button itself is not the feature. The feature is what the button does *when you click it*. Right?

That's worth meditating on.

An economist might call a social network a *coordination mechanism*. All the buttons and features are really just a way to help people do something *together*. Unfortunately, we mostly coordinate to share funny things or buy terrible stock options. But I digress.

From a designer's perspective, social networks combine elements of *entertainment,* because we use them to kill time with fun, and elements of *efficiency,* because their structure and features must make it easy to find relevant content and to buy ads that drive traffic for advertisers.

Social networks and communities are some of the most challenging products to get right, and the key is to focus on real human connections, not just buttons and functionality.

Free Things Can Make a Lot of Money...Eventually

Enough users
to make money

We could have discussed *free* business models more in the section about B2B software, but it's even cooler in the context of a social platform. Let's look at both.

A lot of products and platforms are free for users. They might start free and have a "premium" level you can pay for. Or they might be free forever because someone else is paying. Gmail, for example, is free. Heavy users or business users can pay to upgrade their storage and features, and that revenue is enough to pay for all the free users. That's "freemium." Google's job is to convert enough free users into paying users to pay the bills. On X, everything is free, and users can buy a few premium features, but mostly the bills are paid by advertisers.

Most business models like that actually lose money in the beginning. Investors pay the bills first and hope that *network effects* will drive enough growth to make money someday.

What Are Network Effects, Really?

Heads up, this is important! We briefly touched on *network effects* previously, but now is when we really need them: network effects make a product or platform more valuable when more people use it.

Human connections as a feature are not just an emotional thing. They are also *literal*. Social networks have become so well-known that a lot of people think that *following* or *sharing* are the network effects. I have heard investors describe anything with a "share" button as having *network effects*.

Let's take our bakery, which has zero network effects. More customers does not make my experience of the bakery any better. It might even be worse since I might have to wait in line. But what if I get a discount for referring a friend?

Although that is the weakest possible network effect, it is something. The more customers I bring to the bakery, the less I pay. Less cost = more value. But what if that is a *lifetime* discount of 10%, and I get that for *every* new customer I bring in, forever? Now we're talking.

That is essentially the business model that Groupon uses; the price gets lower every time another person joins a sale. Wouldn't you bring in as many other customers as you could if you could get cakes for $1 for the rest of your life?

X is similar. One user sharing with one other user would be boring: the feed would be empty, and the post quality would be low. And if you don't know that person, who cares, right? The *probability* of your feed showing something interesting is low. But with a *million* users, the probability of *somebody* posting *something* interesting when you log in is much, much higher. More users = more value.

Uber even uses network effects *in reverse* by increasing or decreasing their *prices* depending on demand. More users = *higher* prices! Doing that allows them to *coordinate* users for maximum efficiency.

Network effects are: *connections* between users, designed to *coordinate* those users, in a way that *creates value more efficiently as the network scales.*

Virality Multiplies All of Your Choices *Exponentially*

0.2%

0.1%

Our efficient connections between users (like sharing every post you like with your followers) cause something interesting—virality and exponential growth.

Let's say I post a picture of my legs on a beach. Super amazing, obviously. 0.1% of my 10,000 followers share it, because they have never seen a post like that before (the other 99.9% couldn't care less). And let's say they also have 10,000 followers each, who do the same, as do their followers, and so on.

My post: shared with *10,000 users*. 0.1% = 10 shares.

After the first share: shared with *110,000 users*. 0.1% = 110 shares.

After the second share: shared with *1,110,000 users*. 0.1% = 1,110 shares.

After a couple more shares, my legs would be seen by the population of planet Earth. As they should! That's virality. And that kind of growth is *exponential*. It might start small, but it grows very, very fast. Without a network of connections, that doesn't happen often; on social media it happens daily.

That's why even a tiny design change can have a huge effect. The *probability* of getting one more share matters a lot! The difference between 0.1% and 0.2% becomes enormous!

For social networks, spend most of your time thinking about how to make *better* content travel to *more* people in *less* time. Also, *remove* every detail that might make that process slower. X, Instagram, and TikTok are just an easy post with share buttons, a feed optimized by an algorithm, a search, and a follow button on every profile. In principle, they are pretty simple! But those are the *right* features to achieve virality.

But wait! Be careful: if you *decrease* the probability of content being discovered or *decrease* the average number of posts per user, even a little, you might see large-scale negative effects. When every design choice could launch a nuke, don't just open Figma and bang out a new feature. Take your time.

A What-Not-to-Do Example: Clubhouse

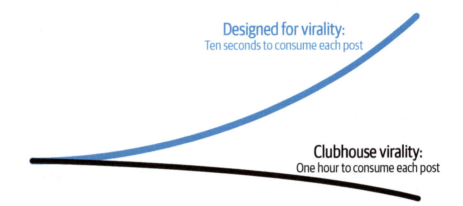

Five minutes after being invited to Clubhouse, a superhot new "audio social network," I saw that it was not the next big social network everybody thought it was during the pandemic. The reason is because of what I just mentioned: it was not designed for *virality*.

When you scroll through the feed on TikTok or Instagram, it takes a few seconds to consume a post and like/share it. Pictures and videos are fast. One user can see a *lot* of posts, and the *probability* of liking or sharing one of them is pretty high. Liking/sharing behavior is *very fast*. But on Clubhouse, it could take *up to an hour* for you to finish listening to a discussion, so each user's liking or sharing behavior is *very slow*.

Clubhouse did a *great* job of launching, though. For a few weeks it was everywhere! But *joining* a social network and *using* a social network are two different things. Ironically, the Clubhouse launch was successful because it spread through *other social networks*, but investors saw that as success for Clubhouse instead of X, etc.

Oops.

How You Monetize Determines Your Problems

Since social networks need a bunch of users to be valuable, they usually start by *not* making money, and then the founders need to figure out how to *monetize* the network after it grows (i.e., how to make money from it). A bakery never has to "monetize"; they just sell cakes on the first day like most traditional businesses.

But *how* you monetize a network-based platform changes a lot.

Similar to the content-heavy business models we discussed before, a social network can sell ads like TikTok and Instagram or subscriptions like Substack and Medium or paid features for premium users, like X has recently introduced.

Ads create situations where you might be *manipulating* users for profit, subscriptions create situations where you might want to pay your best users *less* by taking larger commissions, and premium features make it tempting to have *worse unpaid features*, so the platform becomes unattractive for new free users.

Protecting user value while you *build* business value is hard!

Social Incentives Are Powerful Weapons

Every social network needs a few key social incentives to coordinate the crowd. *Likes* and *followers* are classic examples.

Likes and followers tell the algorithm what each user wants to see and allows people to connect with each other. Without them, a social network wouldn't act like a *network*. But those features do more than just make the network function and grow.

When a feature can give one user an advantage over other users or make a user look good or feel good, it becomes an *incentive*. Users don't just want likes because we told them to. They want likes because of how likes and followers make them *feel*.

We can *design* those incentives and what they motivate people to do. Spotify, for example, shows *monthly listeners* instead of followers. Followers are forever, but on Spotify you need to constantly keep your listeners coming back for more. That's a different incentive! And much more aligned with Spotify's business model.

LinkedIn users were very quick to figure out that the algorithm rewards pretty basic things. Since LinkedIn is mostly used by companies and professionals, there was also a *budget* behind those incentives and nobody was worried about looking superficial. Now we see an avalanche of fake-humble announcements and posts asking users to "vote" with the like button just to be more visible. You see a lot less of that on Facebook because openly fluffing your high school friends for likes somehow doesn't feel as good, and much less of the users see Facebook as employer brand-building.

Social incentives might look like innocent little features, but they are actually very powerful at scale.

Don't Wave That Thing Around; It's Loaded!

When you put 100 million people in one place and reward everyone for doing the same things, you give the whole network a strong reason to do something new. (That's not humans changing; that's just how social behavior works.)

However, each individual will interpret an incentive in their own way. There are a lot of reasons you might want followers. You might have a startup to promote or a cult to grow or a little league baseball team that needs donations. You might just have opinions the world needs to hear.

But just because you have good intentions doesn't mean every user will too. On X, features that were intended to create sharing and connections also gave sexist, racist mobs effective tools for finding and harassing women and minorities. There are negative examples like this from all major networks, ranging from offline witch hunts to political election manipulation. Same incentives, different interpretations!

Remember: every choice you design will be multiplied *exponentially*. Your intentions might be good, but at a large scale it is difficult to anticipate how incentives might motivate someone.

Why Algorithms?

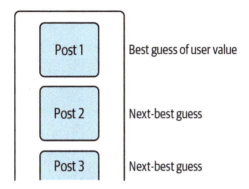

The short answer is: probability!

More and more things in our digital companies are being decided by algorithms. Algorithms don't have to be super smart. They can be really stupid, like, "Every time I click this button, multiply the date by 2 and add that to my salary." However, usually when we say *algorithm*, we mean artificial intelligence or machine learning. Algorithms like that are used to prioritize the vast social content on a network in a way that people could never do.

Imagine if a human being had to decide which content each user would like most. There are *billions* of posts on, say, X. For each one, each time, you would have to consider things like, What does this user like? What have they seen before? Who posted this? What is this about? Did other similar users like it?

It very quickly becomes a task too complex and too subjective for anyone to do with simple rules. Instead, we use an algorithm. To oversimplify, our algorithm might give *points* to each of those factors, and then for each user's feed it will show the user the posts that have the most points each time they log in.

When designing a business or platform like a social network, an algorithm becomes the only way we can handle gigantic volumes of content (posts) that are constantly being made by millions of people.

That being said, algorithms make the experience of each user much, much better than it would be without an algorithm (theoretically, at least) because instead of seeing an unsorted mess of posts, they see a highly curated selection of things that seem likely to be interesting for that user.

The *feed* in all social networks is really an instant list of the posts *most likely* to trigger the valuable actions such as liking and following and sharing, which make the social network work! Probability wins again!

The Probability of Content Creation and Consumption

Speaking of probability, on a social network, if users aren't posting or consuming posts enough, that is something worth your attention. Measure it!

As we discussed earlier, TikTok and Instagram are very efficient that way, and Clubhouse has very limited potential. It's just math! Apps like BeReal, which spontaneously asks users to post a two-minute video, all at the same time, at random times, create a very efficient system. A flood of short posts, and you're not *allowed* to work hard? Perfect.

Let's look at four probabilities:

1. How frequently a user can post (every minute, every day, every year?)

2. How many times a user can post (once, a thousand times, as much as they want?)

3. How long it takes to consume a post (6 seconds, 60 seconds, 60 minutes?)

4. What kind of content is being created (text, images, audio, video, long, or short?)

If the goal is growth, Clubhouse scores badly in all four of those areas. A live, one-hour panel discussion (Clubhouse's main content) is basically a live podcast or a conference talk. That's a lot of work for the poster *and* the listeners! Far too much work for the average user to do very often. I would be exhausted after eight live panel discussions in a day, but eight Instagram posts is something I would do for fun. Long-form, high-quality content creates very loyal users, but that audience will be small, because most people just won't consume enough material to become loyal! Quick, entertaining, superficial content builds large audiences with no loyalty. So, in all four measures, Clubhouse is not designed with scale in mind.

But what if you wanted to fix problems like these? What could you do?

What if you could post a five-minute discussion? What if it wasn't live? What if the live things became small snippets to listen to later? What if the algorithm could curate those snippets around topics? What if you just posted a question and the discussion came in as audio replies instead of a panel, like Quora for audio? These may or may not be good ideas, but they would all theoretically improve probabilities compared to Clubhouse.

Why Most Companies Kill Their Own Communities

I have been the designer of several communities and social platforms in my life, and I have produced significant results in each one. And in each one, the "business" people quickly took it and killed it.

When building a community, the users are not loyal to the *business*. They want to connect and engage *with each other*. And as basic as it sounds, all you really have to do to grow a community is to think like a generous member of it: focus on the *user value* at all times.

A million engaged users have a way of looking like an irresistible opportunity to sell shit. But as soon as a company starts to feel like they *own* the users—smothering them in advertising or making the free version bad to "force" upgrades—it can all come to an end pretty quickly.

As a business, a community isn't something *you* make, it is something you create a place for.

Games and Gamification

Deep Game Design Is Beyond the Scope of This Book

In this section, I want to discuss a few general principles that are broadly useful when we think about designing games as a business. However, to intelligently compare casual games like *Wordle* and *Candy Crush* with serious gaming or esports like *Counter-Strike* and *World of Warcraft*, we would need far more space and experience than I have to offer.

Game design is complex in its own right! But if you zoom out far enough and perhaps take a psychological perspective, the principles are not so different from many of the things we have already seen in this book.

Games Are Entertainment, Not Efficiency

As a general rule, the best games are not designed to be efficient solutions to rational problems. They are supposed to be fun! Later, I will give you a big exception to this.

In fact, one of the core ideas in UX is flipped around in games: they have to be *difficult enough* to be fun! Whether it is a simple mobile puzzle game or a complex set of military missions, the whole idea is to keep increasing the difficulty as you learn and improve! Reverse usability!

Since games are entertainment, we want them to be immersive and to be a place where users can spend as much time as possible. And although they need to be hard enough, games should never be so hard or confusing that the user will give up or lose hope of winning or completing the level or task.

You need to find the sweet spot between challenge and enjoyment. The business part can happen when users are willing to *pay* to experience that feeling.

Quantified Feelings: Games in a Nutshell

You might have noticed that the incentives used in social networks look a little like points in a game. Likes, followers, views, listeners...what do they mean? Nothing! Just like points.

Humans naturally want to win or make progress. It makes us feel good. Although there can be real money value to having more followers and better posts, that's not what really motivates us toward those goals.

It's the feelings.

By turning those actions into points or badges or levels, we can *measure* them; it becomes easier to have *feelings* about them. You can't be happy about your follower count if you don't know what it is!

Gamification turns feelings into a design tool. (With great power comes great responsibility!)

Whether it is basketball or *Counter-Strike* or checkers, when reduced to its simplest form, a game is 1) an emotional goal (winning), 2) a way to measure/compare the players or teams (points), and 3) some rules to make it interesting.

But in business, the *feelings* are the part that everybody forgets...

Gamification

And here is the big exception: gamification, or the idea of making your nongame product feel more like a game, is a good way to get more engagement from an *efficiency problem*. Although the hype of "gamifying" products is not as crazy as it was in the 2010s, the idea of adding "points and badges" to a product is still very much alive.

To use an "oldie but goodie" example: Amazon reviews are gamified. From the outside, all we see is a button that says, "Was this review helpful?" But behind the scenes, those clicks become points in an *extremely* competitive battle royale to be the top product reviewer. A not-so-fun efficiency task (reviewing products) has been successfully turned into a game.

Wikipedia is also a competition behind the scenes, where writers and editors are recognized for their contributions and get status and privileges in return. That (social) game coordinates the users around the enormous task of editing Wikipedia! Amazing!

I have seen examples of people solving problems in biology, medicine, programming, data collection, and many other industries using gamification, even when there was no engagement before!

And really, when you think about it, why do humans care so much about kicking or throwing various balls into various nets? Game psychology is a very large, very profitable industry, and we *love it!*

When gamification *doesn't* work, it's because—yet again—the business forgot that users are people. They add "points and badges," thinking that users will mindlessly start engaging, and they don't. The gamified product still sucks because it didn't quantify any *feelings*.

To make gamification work, first quantify some valuable actions to create points. Then *use* the points (or badges, or levels) to give users good feelings. Turn it into a status symbol or a competition or a prize. For example, I once worked on a game with virtual currency (play money = points), where we rewarded users with a bit of currency for doing a daily task. We used it to promote new features and top users!

The First Taste Is Free

A common pattern in games is to give users something free and/or easy to try as their first experience. In mobile gaming it might be the first few levels before you have to pay, and in business software it might be a free trial, or in a consumer app it might be a guided onboarding experience.

There are at least three good reasons for this approach:

- *Eliminate barriers for the user.* A gentle entry without paying or needing to know anything ensures that as many users as possible get into Level 1.

- *You can't love something you have never felt.* If the experience of your game (or nongame) is good, let the users *feel* it. Don't expect users to love something before they have tried it.

- *Let them feel smart/powerful.* Typically, the first level is really easy or the software is preloaded with a demo account. This lets users feel what mastery is like immediately.

Difficulty Is a Feature

You died.

Try again?

One of the aspects of game design that separates it from other kinds of UX design is how you manage difficulty. In a good game, it is both *easy to use* and *challenging to play*. In other words, usability and difficulty are separate ideas!

Usability is about making the interface understandable and clear and helping the user know how and when to operate the game. It's not the game itself; it's just the navigation of the game.

Difficulty is about the skill of playing the game itself, and ideally it should get harder as the user improves. Fine-tuning the level of difficulty throughout the game is often a key element in the success of a game, and sometimes the hardest games are the best!

When a game is difficult to play because it is hard to use (i.e., poor usability), that's bad and annoying. Frankly, bad usability has probably killed a lot of games that were otherwise interesting.

Match the Business Model to the Structure of the Game

Typically, the quality of the game, rather than the business model, matters most. If the game sucks, it doesn't matter how you plan to make money! But when business starts to matter, the design of the game should determine how users should pay:

- In games where you "beat the game" or sports games that follow real life, users should probably pay to own the game. Once they beat it or real life changes, they will be less motivated to keep paying. Then release updated versions to buy again.

- In games you can play over and over, like *Mario Kart*, players can be engaged long-term, but the risk is that they will eventually get bored. Allow them to buy *more of the game* like new tracks, new characters, etc., as a way to essentially sell the same game again!

- In games that never end, like *Candy Crush*, use a never-ending payment model, like paying to skip hard levels or a subscription to save the progress accumulated over time.

Diagnosis and Probability Depend on the Game

Games, like any product, will have strengths and weaknesses in the design and must be measured and diagnosed, but this is where our general principles start to be a little too general.

We have already discussed some major aspects of games (and gamification) that you will want to look at if users stop playing or lose interest at a certain point in the game: difficulty, usability, payment models, and, most importantly, managing player emotions and experiences.

However, beyond those general ideas, it will depend on exactly what type of game you are working on and how you have designed the incentives. Start with your goals, work backward, measure everything, and gather symptoms as always.

Internal Tools

Captive Users

We have already seen mistakes that happen because businesses forget that users can leave. Now let's look at a group of users who can't leave: employees.

Companies often need to make software and apps to manage their own work. Employees *must* use those tools to do their job. That gives us some opportunities that seem like luxuries compared to normal users.

We can *train* employees, so we can design things that might be hard to use the first time. We don't need to worry about engagement or loyalty because employees have no choice. And they aren't allowed to choose another tool. No more worrying about whether they choose to buy!

Those are all dangerous opportunities. We might fix usability problems with more training, skip our user research because we don't have to make the users happy, and make unnecessary features because complexity won't hurt our user numbers.

Understand What Makes Money, Not Just User Requests

This principle is true for every product or service you design, but when you don't have external users, it becomes critical: understand the problems you are solving, not just the wish list from users. The difference with internal tools is the balance of business value and user value: tip it further toward the business.

When you diagnose the business model to understand how value is created, you should understand the processes that employees follow to do their work. They are the users now, so business value and user value are extremely related!

Instead of following the actions a user takes to get to a buy button or an upgrade button or a share button, you are now interested in the actions that employees take to launch their campaigns or collect their data or manage customer accounts.

Understanding how each employee contributes to the business and *external* user value will teach you about how to create more *internal* value with internal tools.

Internal Tools Should Increase Your Capacity

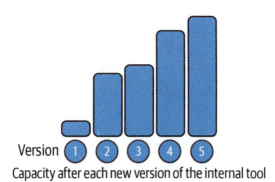

Capacity after each new version of the internal tool

Internal apps and software should make employees more productive. It is the ultimate *efficiency* problem. If you imagine that you are trying to give the employees (your colleagues!) superpowers, it will help you see the right opportunities and avoid lazy temptations.

A hardcore focus on efficiency means identifying the tasks or obstacles that make each employee slow down, wait, or repeat the same manual work over and over. In other words, *bottlenecks*. Every little bottleneck in an employee's work reduces their power to create business value and user value.

If you can remove bottlenecks and tedious work with software, you not only improve efficiency, you avoid *adding* the cost of hiring unnecessary employees. Even better: smaller companies can compete against bigger companies if internal tools allow the smaller teams to produce as much as the bigger, slower competitors.

Employees will give valuable feedback, but don't just ask what they want. Be the expert. Use your skills and knowledge to see the bigger patterns and opportunities they won't ask for.

Avoid the Temptation to Prioritize Yourself

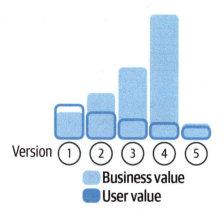

For *internal* software, the company is both the buyer and the user. Twice the reason to do what they want. When a senior manager requests something that will take a lot of resources from the design and tech team, you will be tempted to prioritize that over new features or user research for *external* users.

But it's even harder than that. When you sit beside the users you are designing for or when you see them at the coffee machine every day, their needs will feel very real and urgent compared to the mysterious, distant users outside the company. Especially when your colleagues are happy with your work. We want to hear that sweet, sweet positive feedback!

Prioritize carefully! Be tough about the value you create (or don't).

Someday, if you're launching version 5 of the internal tool and version 2 of your actual product, that's a problem. A balance is healthy, but always prioritize external users when your resources are limited...without them, the internal tool doesn't help anybody.

Protips: Reliable Symptoms

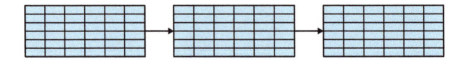

There are a few general things I have seen in real projects that tend to be strong symptoms of valuable problems. If you see those symptoms, I suggest you start digging.

To recognize these symptoms, you should think about the difference between *objective* and *subjective* work. Objective work is made of tasks that do not require much judgement. They are true/false decisions, or more like a recipe. Subjective work is made of hard decisions and judgement calls that only an informed person can make, like communicating with customers or strategic work. *Objective work is often something you can eliminate.*

The first reliable symptom to look for is repetition. If you see employees copy-paste information between documents or enter the same data about customers over and over, there is a good chance that those tasks can be automated or made into a form that customers can fill in directly.

The second reliable symptom is a spreadsheet that is only used by one or a few people. Those are often just people trying to organize themselves or track things that are very objective. The great thing about those spreadsheets is they already contain a lot of information about what you should design or build!

The third symptom is actually a source of information: customer service. Ask them which questions they answer the most. Quite often, you can eliminate the source of that question, and you should!

The fourth symptom is small, common, frustrating human errors. Stuff like typing the wrong name or number. If someone says something like "Ugh! I did it again!"...that's what you're looking for.

If you work at the company you are designing for, then you have a long time to find and analyze symptoms. In every meeting and conversation, you can passively do user research simply by asking yourself, "Could a computer do this faster or make less mistakes?" If the answer is yes, start working on it!

Data Without Significance: Not Enough Users

The biggest weakness you will encounter when working on internal tools is data. Or a lack of data. Throughout this book, I have tried to emphasize how valuable user analytics data is, and I always recommend using it together with user research to diagnose problems and improve probability.

Except when you don't have enough users.

Analytics need to have at least a few hundred users to produce data you can trust. When you work with employees, you might only have 10 or 20 relevant users to measure, so each user has a huge effect on the data. Mathematically speaking, we don't have enough data to reach *statistical significance*. You can't trust the data to be reliable enough.

Without data, you must rely heavily on the *theoretical* background we're discussing in this book. Don't use internal opinions as a substitute for data!

Measure business results instead of user behavior: time per task, production per employee, sales per employee, customer service requests per month, etc.

Machine Learning, AI, and Data Products

AI Is the New Black

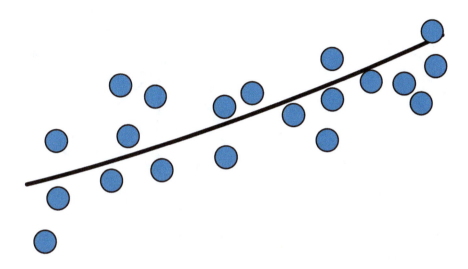

It is quite clear that machine learning and artificial intelligence are here to stay and rapidly expanding. Ten years ago, designers and businesspeople could avoid the complexity of thinking about advanced data solutions, but those days are gone. Ten years from now, any company that ignores AI might not be a company anymore.

In this section, our goal is not to develop a deep understanding of machine learning, but rather to think about how we can design for it and use it to build value in ways that we couldn't do otherwise.

Think: New Speed, Not New Knowledge

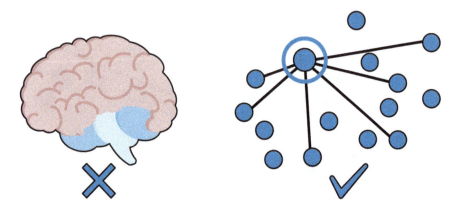

The most dangerous temptation when working with AI is to imagine that it "knows" things it doesn't know.

The best way to think about artificial intelligence is what I often call "fancy counting." An AI model is really just a set of rules about what to count and how to count. It might count the relationships between words or it might give a score to 100 different traits of people based on their movie choices or it might count how much electricity capacity is being used at different places in a city. It can't count what isn't in the data.

The best and funniest description of AI I have seen was when someone said ChatGPT was the "ultimate mansplainer." Ask it anything and it will give you a long and detailed answer, even if it has no idea what it is talking about!

AI can process very complex information and turn it into valuable decisions, but it does not add any knowledge that wasn't somewhere in that data already. Sometimes that is *really* easy to forget.

Data Doesn't Always Mean AI

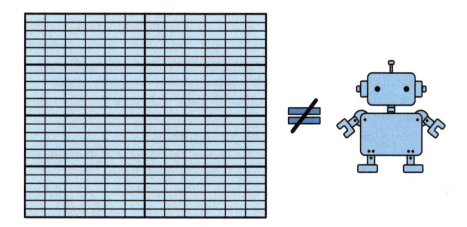

It's very common to reach for the newest, hottest machine learning techniques to solve a problem. You don't necessarily need advanced AI solutions to make your data valuable and useful. Data scientists can contribute very valuable analysis, and engineers can develop fairly simple algorithms that still produce decisions or categories that solve the problem.

Analytics tools, like Google Analytics, for example, might do a lot of work in the background to make your data easy to read and calculate statistics, but you don't need AI to see where your website is performing well or not. In other words, sometimes normal (not so fancy) counting is enough!

There is a whole spectrum of things you can build with and for data, and you should try to design solutions that are only as complex as needed, not more.

And beyond that, don't forget to use the intelligence of your users! Sometimes combining a little AI with the knowledge of the user is the smartest combination; let the computer do the heavy lifting, but let the human decide.

Data for What?

To understand the *value* of data in a product or service, it is critical to understand what your users need data for. What, exactly, do they intend to *do* with the data?

Business users, for example, may not care about the actual data or technology used to deliver that data. They might be mostly focused on insights or performance metrics they get in the interface of the data tool. Like sales numbers. The sales team couldn't care less about the data itself as long as they can manage their deals.

As a very different example, data teams might buy data as a service. The "real" product might be an API that delivers data directly to them in large quantities, and the interface is just a way to explore the data manually.

Those two products should be radically different. Different users, different value, and different uses of the same data. As we learned earlier in this book, when the context changes, the design should change.

Data Quality Is a UX Problem Too

One common issue when designing for data is *data quality*. When you only experience data as the end user, after all the work has been done to clean it, process it, and present it very nicely, you may not realize how inconsistent and generally annoying the data itself was at the beginning.

For example, you might get financial data for a million companies, from the past 10 years. Only 30% of the companies have data for all 10 years, some will only have 1 year, the financials might be in 25 different currencies, and sometimes, randomly, the data might be an error instead of a number. There is no pattern to the missing data, no obvious reason for the errors, and when you're missing the country of the company, you might have to guess which currency it is.

Those are data quality issues. Not the designer's job, but it *is* your job to design a product that handles all of those issues *gracefully*. How would you display 4 out of 10 years of Japanese financials when one of those years is an error? What if you have to show it in the same table as a small American company with 10 years of data, but much smaller numbers in US dollars, and compare those two performances?

Suddenly your simple app that "only" displays financial data looks like quite a lot of work! And it is!

If you don't take special care and spend the time to understand the data quality issues (which might require a lot of collaboration with a data scientist!), you will have no chance of designing good solutions to those issues.

Data quality and UX quality are related problems. And if the data quality makes the data unusable for a user, suddenly the data itself is destroying the user value and business value!

Visualizing Data

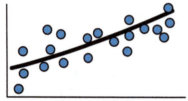

They needed this

You gave them this

There are plenty of examples online of people who design infographics or graphs with *aesthetics* as their main priority instead of information. A pretty graph is always nice to see, but if users can't make sense of it, what are you really doing?

Two very easy mistakes are the reason for almost every bad data visualization I have ever seen: 1) you don't understand the numbers yourself, so you do something ridiculous to make them look good, or 2) you don't understand your audience (users), so you make it too easy or too complex for them.

That's it! There are entire books about visualizing data, and if you visualize data often, read one! They will help you choose the *correct* way to present data, like not putting things in a pie chart if they don't add up to 100%. Rookie mistake!

But even then, when you screw up it will be something lazy and pretty, or something for the wrong audience.

Controlling and Confirming Bias

When you are the provider of data, like many data software and tools can be, you actually have the power to lie to your users by accident. If your users are investors, for example, they might spend millions or billions of dollars based on those lies.

A rather big problem, I would say. Because the lie isn't what you say; it's what you *don't* say.

When we deliver or present data, we might be giving users a *bias*. A bias is a preference or an assumption or something else that might affect the way data is *interpreted* by the user. The problem is even worse when you help the user believe something they *want to believe*! If it isn't true, they might not even *want* to check it.

Here are three examples to avoid:

- *Bias in data we have processed.* When data companies "fix" data quality issues or calculate things for the sake of showing insights in the data, sometimes they make choices that are not obvious to the user. At my company, we have found several of these types of biases in data that is precalculated from data providers—sometimes with dramatic results!— and we've had to recalculate everything from scratch instead. But it took weeks of work to find them!

- *Bias in the presentation.* One classic example of displaying data in a biased way is starting the y-axis (the vertical numbers on the graph, usually on the left side) at a number that isn't zero. That can make a subtle change seem like a big change visually.

- *Algorithm bias.* This is becoming more and more of an issue. It is common for the programmers to include their own biases in the artificial intelligence model without realizing it, or *training* the AI with biased data. That's how we get algorithms that are racist or AI that sounds credible but is actually incorrect.

Controlling bias is a subtle thing. Search for "cognitive biases" and spend some time understanding the ways humans make predictable mistakes, especially with numbers. Then try to help users avoid those mistakes wherever you can.

If You Aren't Comfortable with Numbers, Don't Take the Job

I have been talking a lot about understanding the data yourself and knowing a little about the statistics you're designing. I *highly* recommend building your own confidence in these things.

But...

If you just hate numbers or if you really don't feel comfortable with numbers, you become a risk when working with data. Lots of designers get into design from the "art" side of things, so I would never blame a designer for not having an interest in the analytic side, but when you work with data products directly, that becomes a real problem.

Best case, the developers won't take you seriously, and they will keep you away from numbers. Worst case, you will design things that are just wrong mathematically, and they will build them anyway.

I recommend learning as much as you can about everything you design, including data.

User Research About Data Is Data!

When the product is data, for some reason it is quite common to think that *user research* isn't important anymore. Au contraire! It is just as important, if not more important!

Since data is so objective and complex and the users are often programmers and the product might be the data itself...we might not get the same kind of "soft" feedback we might get otherwise.

Doing user research for data-oriented products puts more responsibility on you, the researcher. Aim for a deeper understanding of the *context* where the data is used on the user's side. What is the *real* value of this data for the customers? Investors and marketers might want the exact same SEO data, but they will do entirely different things with it.

And you should be able to get a lot of good *user data* about how people use the product! Whether it is in an interface or an API, almost everything will be measurable and very valuable when you understand context well.

Does Anybody Even Want the Truth?

I have had a lot of questionable requests related to data. Usually something like this:

> Guy: Joel, can you get me some data that says this campaign was a success?
>
> Me: Was it a success?
>
> Guy: Nah, it wasn't great, but I can't say that to the client.
>
> Me: Then I think we should talk about how to explain the results, not how to lie about it.

A manager once asked me to make the software biased toward his work. I have been told *not* to include negative insights because they will make bosses say no to a proposed project (the project happened and was a disaster). And I have literally been told to change the data in a presentation to make it better!

I didn't do those requests. I was replaced on the disaster project (dodged a bullet, in my opinion!)

Always be helpful, but *think very hard* before you intentionally use data to lie. Feeling good about manipulated data doesn't make the data correct. The consequences can be very real.

Ecosystems

What Is an "Ecosystem"?

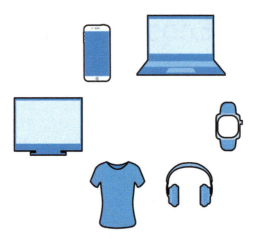

To be honest, *ecosystem* is not a word with one good definition. So far in this book, most of the conversation has been about *one* product or service, and for most companies, that is all the complexity you need in your life. Even two or three products may not be related to each other in a way that is difficult to manage.

Ecosystems happen in *big companies*, usually.

An *ecosystem* (in this book, at least) is a collection of products and services that are designed to *work together* as a group. A customer can enter the ecosystem by using *any* of those products and services, and when they do, it improves the chance of using *every* other product or service in the ecosystem.

When we learned about the *structure* of pages earlier, the big idea was to design how users move through that structure so the *value* is easier to access.

Now we will use the same idea *across* products and services instead of *within* one product.

Probability *Still* Defines Structure!

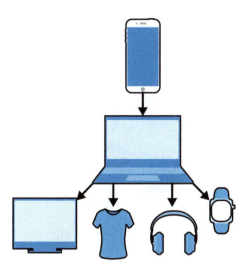

When we think about *probability* in the context of multiple products or services, we can think about it from a few different starting points: which product people use most, which products we *want* them to use most, and which products make sense to use *next*.

Let's say you have a main product and two smaller products, just for example. Most people use the main product, and you make most of your money from it. You want your main product to act like the connector between the smaller ones, and you don't have to worry as much about connecting the smaller products to each other. (It's a "nice to have," not a "must-have.")

Even if you have 10 smaller products and services, or 100, it is usually wise to structure the ecosystem so a few products get all the attention, like Google Search, while all the other products just do a good job of "plugging into" those main products (like Google Workspace, Google Finance, Google Analytics, Google Chrome, and so on).

VDP Still Applies!

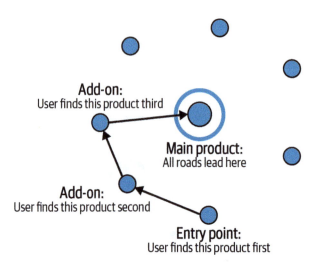

Value, diagnosis, and probability! Zoom out and think about your products and services like one big set of connected tools. You should still be able to follow a user or a use case through those tools as a *chain*. When I log in to Google Sheets, use Google Finance to get stock data, and then search for that company in the search bar of Google Chrome, I arrive in Google Search results. As a user, that feels intuitive, but behind the scenes, a lot of products are working together, exactly when I need them!

If we get a lot of feedback and data that indicates users get lost somewhere in that sequence, we can follow the *value chain* backward from Search to Sheets, looking for clusters of symptoms to form a diagnosis.

And somewhere in there, business value should be created too! We want that Google Sheet to motivate a business subscription or sell clicks in the Search results or at least collect good data to make Search more intelligent. Or reduce costs!

VDP. On a large scale.

Strategy: What Kind of Ecosystem Do You Need?

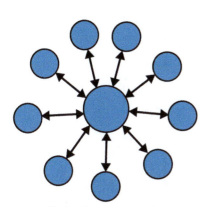
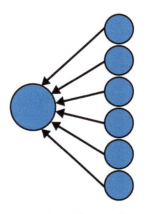

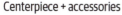
Centerpiece + accessories   Revenue engine with supporting services

Google and Apple both have good, but different, ecosystem strategies.

Google puts Search in the center and a long list of other products around that, which might make some money, too, but the primary goal is to create data and traffic to drive Search. (It's more complicated than that, but let's keep this simple.) Google products are open, often free, and in general they want the whole world to use Google *by default*.

Apple uses a "walled garden" strategy. Unlike Google, Apple's rather expensive *devices* are at the center, and basically worshipped from a marketing perspective. Once you own an iPhone or a MacBook, all of Apple's well-designed software, apps, and *other* devices work together and seem more practical. Competitor devices, such as an Android phone (made by Google), are more effort for the user. Apple charges more for that convenience, because they can, and Google charges less to attract a broader audience.

Both good strategies! Both are designed to build on the strongest probabilities: search for Google and hardware for Apple.

Brand Ecosystem

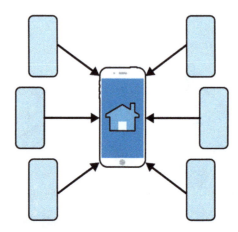

Branded online/offline touchpoints drive visitors to the main brand experience

Another style of ecosystems is when a company is brand-driven, instead of product-driven. A company like Coca-Cola or Nike or Absolut Vodka focuses heavily on *brand* assets. Unlike Google's search or Apple's computers, soft drinks and shoes and alcohol are easily replaceable, so branding is critically important.

In brand-driven companies, you will often see ecosystems of "touchpoints" instead of products or services. Touchpoints are different places the customer can make contact with the brand, like their website, social media profiles, events, advertising campaigns, stores, and so on. A brand ecosystem should treat touchpoints the same way we treat products and services in Google's or Apple's ecosystem or how we treat *pages* in a website. Structure and probabilities!

Typically, the brand's main website is in the center, but lately it wouldn't be weird for a social media profile to be the centerpiece. Or an app! You could also drive different audiences to different destinations if the strategy is sophisticated.

One way or another, the brand *properties* should be linked in a structured way, based on probabilities.

Ecosystem Value Can Be Very Indirect

If you're managing a large portfolio of products or sub-brands, you can't expect every piece of the ecosystem to be a big profit machine. It is important to understand how each product or brand property contributes to the whole. It's similar to the purpose of each page of a website: some pages have a Buy button and generate business value directly, but pages like the privacy statement are just there to support other pages indirectly.

At Tesla, the screen in the car might not generate revenue *directly* (if they have launched a big in-car app store when you read this book, pretend they haven't), but the screen contributes a lot to sales just being there and looking good!

The UX of a digital device used for medical surgeries might not generate money directly, but it might contribute to not killing people, which is definitely a big value driver for the business!

Your social media account or the free apps that support the main brand, or a special use case of the product might not be something you *sell* directly, but they might be how you make your customers loyal in between purchases or tell them about new features when they are already users.

Free Gmail users might not create any money themselves, but a certain percentage of those users will buy Google Workspace subscriptions, and the reputation of Gmail as the big, default email provider will help *a lot* when it is time for a company to choose their company email provider. The reputation *indirectly* motivated a big sale!

All of these indirect value-creating products, services, and features don't make or break the business alone, but when combined to support the main products and services that *do* generate most of the money, the ecosystem has a large effect, either to attract new customers or to keep existing ones.

Good ecosystems create an *environment* where it is easier to stay or buy *inside* the ecosystem than *outside*. Or they make it possible to do things that competitors can't match, like offering valuable services for free (which both Google and Apple do).

A Note About Strategy

The word "strategy" is widely abused. Many people struggle to explain their company's strategy. Every time someone says, "Our strategy is to be the best [...] in the world," I throw up a little in my mouth.

The more we talk about the "helicopter view" of a business, the more you are talking about your strategy. It is the *direction* of the business, how your company creates competitive advantages, and how all the parts work together.

Strategy is the big ideas or insights that *unify* and *motivate* all of your plans and work overtime. Any business activities, including design, product, and marketing, that do not align with the bigger strategy are not contributing value to that strategy.

Apple's strategy includes design leadership and their "walled garden" ecosystem as part of what you might call a "luxury" or "premium" strategy. In a word: exclusivity. It affects the way they talk, the stores they build, and the partners they choose. Samsung's strategy is to actively be the strongest #2 company, so they might copy things that Apple does, but more efficiently, and target a broader audience at a better price. *Together* Apple and Samsung capture a big part of all customers, but they both have good strategies. The *differences* in strategies give both companies advantages that are very profitable. If they both did the same things in the same ways, one would lose. How they apply those strategies to every detail of the company are just details in the bigger picture.

If you don't know what your company's strategy is or if you are not working toward the same strategy, then there is a good chance you are just randomly making decisions in your designs. You might *think* you are creating value, but it might be the *wrong kind of value!*

Strategy is the ultimate answer to *why* and *how* your company creates value. Be a part of that strategy.

Meta Design: Design According to Your Problems

"Your Process" Isn't One Process. Be Flexible.

The temptation to be *lazy* when solving problems is always there and always a factor.

I started this book by talking about all the lazy boot camps and UX courses and teachers who try to make it sound like design is one process (often illustrated as two diamonds) that can be applied to all situations. Although that might be reasonable as an abstract concept, in reality your design process will (and should) adapt to what you're working on.

Keep the principles of VDP, but apply them differently depending on the problem and the context.

Only Consider Solutions You Have Researched *First*

The more experience you have, the more often you will see a potential solution quickly. It might look like something you have worked on before, or it might remind you of something you read about. But every company, product, customer, and context comes with its own constraints, limitations, and opportunities.

Resist that urge to build that first idea. Do the research anyway.

A well-researched solution has a lot less risk in it. If you *assume* that everything looks like that other solution you were already familiar with, there is a chance you are wrong. Even if your research *confirms* that you were right, now you *know*! Knowing is always better than assuming.

Saying "always research first" might sound like the opposite of "always adapt your process to the problem," but in fact, *research* is not predefined. It is *how* you know where you should adapt your process, because research is how you understand the problem.

Dogfooding: The Best Research Method Nobody Uses

Imagine a company that makes software for project management, but they use a competitor's software to manage their own projects internally. Do they really *experience* their customer's pain, or is it more of a hypothetical pain, because they use another tool? I propose that they will never *deeply* understand their own product because they use something else.

The expression "eat your own dog food" probably refers to some over-eager dog food manufacturer testing their own product back in the day. Today, "dogfooding" refers to using your own products and services. Not as a test user, not in a staging environment, but as a *real user*.

I know a company that makes an app for anglers (people who fish with a hook). The employees are highly encouraged to start fishing. Why? How can you *truly* understand fishing if you don't fish?!

Another common expression in tech is something like "solve your own problem." That's good, too, but not quite the same. If you start a company to solve a problem you *already had*, that's great. You are already dogfooding. But dogfooding is the idea of *giving yourself the customer's problem* so you can experience it *directly*.

In my entire two-decade-plus career of creating products and services, nothing has ever given me more insights than *becoming* a customer myself, for real. Whether that is a $2 purchase to test a coupon app or a trip to the pharmacy to buy tampons or mixing cocktails at home or investing my own money in real stocks to understand my investor clients, dogfooding provides an *emotional* depth to your research that nothing else can.

If you make project management software and you don't manage your own projects with it, you're missing *a lot*.

Dogfooding Should Be Uncomfortable

If dogfooding your own solutions is so great, then why doesn't everybody do it? Why would a project management software company *not* use their own product, you might say?

Because it's harder. And that's why it's valuable.

If a customer can choose Google's free, finished project management software, or your unfinished, not-so-free project management software, that seems like an obvious choice. When you also use Google's free software while developing your own, you *are actually making that choice* too.

By *forcing* yourself to choose your own (inferior) software, you are causing pain for yourself and suddenly will be *very motivated* to fix that pain! You will not focus on little details or irrelevant copywriting or your 10-year vision anymore, because those things don't fix your pain. That's how your users feel!

Fixing pain = creating value.

It is *remarkable* how fast your deep, personal feelings will align with your customers the moment you feel their pain for yourself. Every moment of every day becomes *research*. Every conversation becomes *prioritized*.

Uncomfortable is good.

Don't Pass the Buck

If we're talking about your design process, we should also talk about *avoiding* your design process. This usually happens when you, the designer or decision maker, are faced with tough choices. Instead of making those choices, you move that responsibility onto someone else so it becomes their problem. The user, for example.

Let's say you can design something two ways, each choice having pros and cons. As the designer, you *could* make the tough choice, but then you would spend a few more hours explaining those choices to stakeholders, and your life will be slightly more annoying. Instead, you could specify *both* solutions! Either a developer will be forced to build both and add complex logic to decide which version each user gets, or you could make it a *setting* that the user must choose for themselves.

Don't do either of those. Those aren't design choices; they are just a designer trying to avoid their own job.

How to Prioritize

VDP Is a Great Way to Prioritize Your Work

Never discuss work in terms of "good" or "bad" ideas. That is a sure sign that you are prioritizing based on stupid criteria.

If you search for "prioritization frameworks," you will find many. They are just ways of deciding what is important now and what isn't, and most are very academic or complex. In my experience, simple methods are usually better in practice.

VDP is everything you need for prioritizing your work:

> *V = Value.* Creating new value is extremely...uh...valuable. Luckily it is also rare. So, when you have a well-researched opportunity to create real value, you should prioritize it first. Most good products will usually only create *fundamental* value in two or three ways, at most. The rest is details and supporting features.

> *D = Diagnosis.* Once you have the fundamental blocks of value in place, the next most valuable thing you can do is make them work *properly*, for example, taking your product from a beta test version to a real *version one*. Diagnostic work tends to add a lot of value and increase business results enough that other people will notice but doesn't create new *types* of value.

> *P = Probability.* When you are creating value and have diagnosed most of the "big" issues and your product is running smoothly (version 2 or 3, for example), the longer-term work will focus more on improving probabilities. Better conversion rates. Selling more per customer. More ways to navigate. And so on. Probability work improves a business *a lot* over time, but each change might be small. So, it should happen a lot, especially on mature products, but it should not be prioritized over new value or diagnosing big issues.

And that's it! *Value. Diagnosis. Probability.* In that order!

One critical thing, though. Creating new value is like planting a seed. Over time, it becomes a tree. Don't plant 100 seeds unless you have the resources to maintain a whole orchard. Plant one seed, take care of it until it becomes a promising young tree (or it fails to grow), and *then* plant another seed, if you can.

The Value of a Feature

Maybe VDP is great for prioritizing on the road map level of planning (months or years), but what about prioritizing next week? How should we choose between two things with similar value or very different benefits?

No matter what anyone says, in real life, you usually won't have a solid answer, and you will make a lot of judgement calls. Often, you will have to make "trade-offs" where you do easier things that are less valuable, and less valuable things that take longer. And that can be a wise thing to do in reality. In fact, "making good trade-offs" is a skill that a lot of managers look for when recruiting, because it must be learned through experience.

The value of a feature is often a matter of...wait for it...probabilities!

Probabilities for the user are a good start: How many users will use it? How often? For how long? What is the cost or pain if you don't make this change? How will they solve it without your change? (For example, will they leave?)

If you have two features that are relatively equal but one of them will be used daily and one of them will be used rarely, build the daily one first. The *probability* of making an impact is higher.

Time and cost are often good criteria for prioritizing, but always compare with the *value*. The more value created, the more time is "worth it." If you prioritize *only* with time and cost, you will eventually have a huge product made of a million tiny, not-so-valuable features, and it will take a year to redesign.

And finally, what about the business? Sometimes building things will not really affect users much, but it will allow the company to do a lot more in the future. Refactoring code, for example, doesn't do anything differently, but it might make all future work 25% faster! Make time for it!

V Then D Then P

The time you spend on design work should depend on the value of that work.

Value creation is the most valuable type of work you can do. Spend time on it. Deep user research should be done before you decide to move forward with a value-creation project, because whether you are right or wrong, it's important.

Diagnostics are the next most valuable projects, so spend plenty of time on diagnosis, but not nearly as long as you might spend creating the fundamental value above.

Probability work, in real life, is either ignored or *way* overdone. Although small tweaks can add up to big value over time, each tweak is small, so they should also be fairly quick.

Value projects take months or years. Probability projects should be days or weeks, max.

Design in Different Situations

Designing with No Budget

"No budget" can come in different flavors. You might be a big company with limited resources, a very small team (maybe one person!) with too much to do, or even a startup that literally has no money for anything!

Ultimately no budget means you can't buy anything external and your internal resources are tight. That means *time* is the resource you should optimize, which means "value per hour" of effort is your priority. In other words, what is the most value you can create with your very limited time?

Research is a good use of time, and you should focus your research on identifying *one* new way to create value or *very few* big issues to solve. Then solve the ones that will actually *deliver* that value as soon as possible (optimize for time!).

The more value you can deliver sooner, the better your chances of generating a "budget" in the future!

Designing with a Huge Budget

With great budgets come great responsibilities. Although lots of junior designers dream of unlimited budgets to do wild and crazy things, in reality a big budget (or a lot of funding) can become an unexpected burden and a source of big, dumb mistakes.

Ironically, when people have no budget, they are careful about how they spend it. But with a huge budget, people start *wasting* their money (and time) much more than they should. Instead of doing a good job of research, they build 100 different things without doing any research. *Don't fall into that trap!*

The best way to manage a big budget is the same as managing a small budget: prioritize value creation, not the quantity of output. The upside of a big budget is not *how much* you can do, but rather the *possible solutions* you can consider. You can get better people or buy outside resources (like data or consultants) too!

Save your budget for when you need it, or when you need it, you might not have any left!

Designing with a Tight Deadline

Let's assume that there is no "extra time" and you have a reasonable budget. There are two big considerations: the scope and which came first (the deadline or the egg).

Don't set a deadline *before* you know what you're trying to make before that date (scope), unless you have no choice. Plans have a way of taking longer than you think in real life, which brings us to the second consideration: if you *must* finish before an ambitious deadline, plan to do *less* than you *can*.

In other words, on a tight deadline, aim to do a good job of a *small* scope. Say no to everything except the essential things.

Doing a terrible job of too much is bad for everyone. Doing a great job of not-quite-enough shows what you can do, making future work and user expectations less stressful.

If you have no time *and* no budget, either work night and day to perform a miracle or go back to the stakeholders and suggest a more reasonable plan.

Designing with No Deadline

It has been said that the longer a project has been going, the *longer* it will keep going. That means a quick project will be a little late, and a huge project may never end! The lesson there is: a few short projects are better than a long one. And in reality, that tends to be true.

Working without any natural end to the project or any expectations about deadlines takes *time* out of the equation and puts a lot more pressure on the *personalities* of the people working on the project (including you).

If you are the kind of person who has lots of discipline and will work efficiently anyway, then no worries. However, if you are a real human being, try to break the work into reasonable iterations or phases, each with their own little deadline, so you can deliver sooner and smaller. Although it might seem counterintuitive, you will do more if you work in smaller pieces and will feel better by achieving milestones.

Designing with Total Freedom

This is another "problem" that many younger designers wish for. Ironically, when you become a senior designer and actually get a project with "creative freedom," the first thing you will do is start adding requirements. Every time I have ever been given carte blanche by a client (which often comes with a large budget too), me and my team have always started looking for valuable problems to solve.

Yes, VDP is a good method even when you can do anything you want.

In fact, the one time I was able to work with no rules at all (the client brief was one line), we made it pretty hard on ourselves, and the results were really good.

The best designers are very skilled at identifying smart *constraints* and valuable *problems*. Creativity is much harder without limitations.

Designing with Strict Limitations

OK, so now I have argued that limitations make you more creative. What about when there are a *lot* of limitations? Touché!

If you think about it, most puzzles and puzzle-style games have extremely strict rules. A crossword puzzle leaves no room for interpretation. And yet, still fun! Approach strict limitations like a puzzle. *Assume* there is an answer that meets *all* of the requirements and start there.

You can also evaluate the limitations to decide which ones are *hard* (like technical requirements), which are *soft* (like stakeholder requirements), and which are actually *open to interpretation* (like user feedback). Also, consider the *value* of each limitation. Some requirements will destroy the business if you don't solve them, and some will just annoy one stakeholder. If you have to sacrifice something, start with the *open* and *low value* requirements.

Some of your most ingenious ideas will come from strict limitations, I promise! Also, coffee.

Designing with Painful Legacy

Eventually in your career, you will work somewhere where new designs and ideas must be compatible with the 20- or 30-year old garbage they keep in the attic. Old systems, code, contracts, customers, and "custom" things sold in the past—all examples of *legacy*. No joke: legacy systems make good people quit; you're not alone.

You will be tempted, as I have been, to "strongly recommend" a total redesign from scratch, just to get something done. However, in reality, that often requires long-term resources and large-scale disruption of day-to-day operations, so good luck with that!

There is no silver bullet for legacy issues, but my advice is: take the time to *really* understand what the legacy is made of and why. Don't accept the answers you get until you get to the root of each one. I was once told by *everyone* at a bank that the lawyers wouldn't allow my idea, and when I asked the lawyers, they loved it!

(And no matter how bad *your* problems seem, the developers probably have it worse!)

Designing for Growth Versus Revenue

Throughout this book, I have often assumed that your company wants to make profit (at least eventually). However, it might surprise you to know that some companies *don't care about that!*

What?! Wait, wait...how can that be? If you live in Silicon Valley, you're probably already with me; but for everybody else, sometimes the best way to get more money from *investors* is to get as big as you can, as fast as you can, even if that means you burn money like an arsonist in a bank vault.

To adjust your process for *growth* rather than *revenue*, simply take costs out of the equation and limit your definition of "value" to the core user acquisition mechanism.

Let me break that down a little more. "User acquisition" is how you get new users or customers. And usually there is one or a few key mechanisms for getting more users. Social networks often have an "invite a friend" function. Business software often has a way to share with or add more users to your account. Or it might just be large-scale advertising and a good registration form!

Your whole life should revolve around that user acquisition mechanism and any essential features that support it. The bigger you actually grow, the more you can expand your attention beyond that mechanism.

Uber, for example, still doesn't make a profit, but they are a worldwide company with hundreds of millions of customers paying for and loving the service. They have excellent mechanisms for matching drivers and passengers, taking payments, and optimizing prices. They achieved that with *billions* of dollars from investors who are betting on a future where Uber can be profitable, somehow (e.g., self-driving cars).

A lot of startups destroy themselves by thinking like this! Growth at all costs is a risky bet; if those companies fail to raise another big round of funding from investors, they often can't afford to operate, and will die!

When this approach works, it is exciting just trying to keep up! When it doesn't, it can be very depressing.

Designing from Scratch

This is probably my favorite scenario to design: starting from nothing. Zero to one. A *huge* responsibility. Similar to total creative freedom, designing a product, service, or company from scratch might seem like an opportunity to do anything you want, but in reality it is the ultimate challenge to give yourself constraints.

Designing from scratch means you have the responsibility to create *value* from zero, which means you have to define the *problem* from zero. And that means research. Designing from scratch means all of your priorities are research-based, because you can't create value if you don't know what problem you're solving.

To be confident that you are solving a *real* and *valuable* problem, you need many good reasons to believe that problem is real and valuable. Remember earlier when we learned about the *value of a problem?* There is no time when that is more useful than when you are designing from scratch.

Look for problems that affect a lot of people, often. Or problems that cost a lot or last a long time when they happen. In a perfect world, you want a problem that costs a lot of people a lot of money or pain, often, and lasts for a long time.

But that's only the *internal* view of the problem. You also need to know who else is solving the problem! Because you don't just have to solve it, you have to solve it better, faster, cheaper, or differently than they do.

To design from scratch, your process is three things:

1. Find a valuable problem and have a lot of evidence that the problem is real.

2. Find a unique way of solving that problem so you have a competitive advantage.

3. Prioritize the hell out of your choices. Build as little as you can, but solve as much as you can, at the same time.

And if you're creating a whole company from scratch, like a startup, this is the only part of this book that you truly need.

VDP Cheat Sheet

Value Creation

Understand the essential steps that create value and make those work first:

1. *Identify your problem(s).* If you don't know what problem you're solving or how you will create value for the user, don't go further. Use the diagnostic process to observe the real world you are working in to identify a valuable real-world problem that really, truly exists among real users—not just something you would like to be better.

2. *Map out the business model.* These are the steps required to turn the inputs of the business (money, people, ingredients, information, technologies, etc.) into the outputs of the business (baked goods, subscribed users, articles, new vehicles, or whatever you are trying to make). Keep in mind that you might be solving a problem that is not well understood yet, so experiment or do research to figure out what the best business model looks like. It can be a challenge, but also pretty fun. And you might even innovate something new!

3. *Think about the money.* After you have a rough idea of how you will create value for the user, give some thought to how you might get paid for that value. Ads? Subscription fees? Premium features? An ecosystem of apps? Somehow, you need to solve the business needs. If you're making a social or viral thing, maybe you can decide later, but it's still good to consider it now.

4. *Solve backwards.* Your business model/user experience journey map (step 2) should include at least one, maybe several, key paths to creating value. Ecommerce stores have one, usually; and complex platforms probably have a few. Regardless of how many, start at the end, when the value is literally created in that moment, and figure out everything needed in that moment to execute the transaction, create the account, or whatever. Then go back one step and figure out what you need in *that* step. And then the step before that one. And so on until you get to the first time a user becomes aware of your company or their problem.

5. *Get some sleep.* You're crushing it. Also, real value creation is usually a big, long, valuable piece of work, and it is worth all the time you put into it. Big value, big effort. Small value, small effort. However, you will rarely create big value overnight, so pace yourself.

Diagnostic Design

Most of your UX work in real life will be diagnostic:

1. *Does it work?* In the real world? With real users? And you can measure that objectively? Great! Start collecting information. Set up analytics, start a routine of meeting users to see how they use your designs, gather feedback from everyone who will talk to you, and try not to spend too much money doing all of that.

2. *Keep a clustered list of observations/symptoms.* Get in the habit of hunting for observations about users and trying to cluster them. The more symptoms that seem to have a common cause, the more likely it is that you have found a valuable problem. If the data shows a drop in conversion, users seem confused, and stakeholders have asked for a bunch of extra required questions in the form on that page...that sounds like a cluster of issues with a common cause.

3. *Start with the most likely causes of the biggest clusters.* Think of as many realistic causes for every cluster of symptoms on your list. When you see a big cluster (many symptoms) and you can imagine a very believable cause for those symptoms, it's time to design something.

4. *Design and test a solution.* When you have designed a new-and-improved solution to the problem causing all of those symptoms, test it in the real world. Ideally, do an A/B test or launch it and measure what users do. Worst case (or if it is not measurable), talk to users and look for reasons it *isn't* working. Remember, you *want* it to work, so try to prove it isn't working. If that is hard to prove, you're probably doing OK!

5. *Win or learn.* If your design has solved the problem, the symptoms should disappear or decrease, or to put it positively, you should see users doing a lot more of what you/they wanted. If not, then you have learned that the most believable cause of the problems *was not the cause*, or your design didn't actually solve the problem. That is valuable information! Start again and either design a solution to the next most likely cause or design a better solution and try another test.

Don't be afraid to spend your time doing the diagnostic work. It isn't always obvious, but it is always valuable when you find a good cluster with a solvable cause.

Probability

Increase the chance of users doing more of the right things and less of the wrong things:

1. *Start with flows and structures.* Even during the first few versions of your designs, you should think about how your flows (sequences of pages) and structures (groups of linked pages) will make users move through your designs. Since it gets harder and harder to change fundamental structures when the product or service gets big, probability should always be in the back.

2. *Structure your designs so big value is close to big defaults, and small value farthest away.* Most users will land at the top of the start page or first app screen by default; therefore, you should put the most valuable features, navigation, or content as close to that screen as possible. The farther a user has to navigate or scroll or search away from that default (first page, at the top), the less likely it is a user will ever see it, so make sure those are things that don't add much value anyway.

3. *This is true on any scale!* A single page can be structured so the most value is most visible, and in an ecosystem of products and services like Apple, the highest probability products will get all the hype, and more niche, specialized products and services will be treated like add-ons to the hyped stuff. What's at the front of the Apple store, near the one big door (the default)? The newest most expensive phones and computers, made by Apple. What's at the back near the cash register? The small accessories, made by third-party vendors. Same idea, different context. That little bit of probabilistic design is probably worth billions every year.

4. *Move constructive actions to the front and destructive actions to the back.* Constructive actions that *add* value or *protect* value in the business model should be first, at the top, or otherwise easiest to find, available wherever there are needs, and close to the defaults. Destructive actions that *remove* or *destroy* value should be last, at the bottom, and hard to click accidentally but should still be relatively easy to find when the user wants them.

5. *Prioritize and estimate value based on how many users will use something, how often, and at what cost.* If five people will use something once per year, the probability of that feature is low in general. If a million people will use something every day, the probability of that feature is very high. It

doesn't matter if the feature is a detail or a big deal, if it is used with high probability, it creates or destroys a lot of value when everything is added together. Use your time on high-value, high-probability problems, features, and anything that deserves a high-probability location in the structure.

6. *With a lot of users, think in smaller probabilities.* A problem that affects 1% of 100 million users can still be a real big problem. It affects a million people! If you're dealing with huge numbers of users or if you have mostly worked with smaller numbers of users, remember that everything happens more often when you're talking about more people, and vice versa: a 1% problem with 100 users is probably not the best thing you could be working on.

Bounce back and forth between diagnostics and probability, and don't be afraid to solve both kinds of problems in one design. The more you practice your VDP thinking, the more you will be able to anticipate probabilities and solve them "while you're in there."

The Who

Company Culture Versus You

It's Not You, It's Them (Probably)

When I was starting to write this book, I asked a group of my senior UX friends, most of whom have worked in very large enterprises more than me, "What do you think designers need to know about working with other people?"

Their answer surprised me.

Rather than saying anything about stakeholders or taking feedback or collaboration, they all gave me some version of "don't take a job if the company culture works against you." They had different perspectives on that idea, such as not working for companies that don't respect you as a person, not working at companies where your personality is a bad fit for the company's values, or not staying at a company if you don't agree with what they do ethically—but they all went there first.

When I asked a little more, they explained that many people, especially younger or inexperienced people, don't have enough experience (professionally or maybe in general) to realize that *it's not their fault*. They will continue to work at terrible jobs or in cultures that totally clash with their own lives or characters because they think *they* are the part that isn't working.

So, although this whole section deals with all the ways you can gain or struggle with various people and stakeholder situations, keep that in mind: sometimes, you should consider leaving or not taking a job in the first place.

"How Do I Persuade Stakeholders?"

The question I get most is definitely this one, so let's spend some time on it. I wish there was a simple, satisfying answer, but there isn't. The best answer is everything you have read in this book so far.

A lot of designers approach stakeholders by trying to *convince* stakeholders to do what *the designer* has already decided, for design reasons. But instead of doing all your work first and then bringing design into their world, do the opposite. Bring their world into your design first, as requirements and *stakeholder research*, and you might be surprised how persuasive you suddenly become.

Stakeholders are the users of *your work* rather than your *designs.* Use the VDP approach: understand what creates value for them, diagnose their problems, and increase the probability of *their* success when you design solutions.

When you can also explain the business reasons for your choices, the measurements of your changes, and say "I don't know" when you haven't solved something yet, stakeholders will learn to trust you.

That's how you persuade stakeholders.

You Don't Have to Explain *Everything*

Often, when designers are struggling to get "buy-in" from stakeholders, it's because they are 1) getting lost in the details, 2) doing design for its own sake, or 3) trying to get permission when they don't need it.

Stakeholders are usually not designers and are often not even product or marketing people. People who know design already understand its value, and people who aren't designers don't have the right background to understand all the details and nuances you have solved during your design process.

Either way, they don't need all the details. Stick to the big insights, the fundamental choices, and the value you are creating (or costs you are eliminating). When you bury your audience in details, it's hard for stakeholders to say yes.

Designers often explain design choices as if the reason for making those choices is "because of design." If you're not motivating your solutions with user needs, business needs, or stakeholder needs, ask yourself, Do you know why you're doing it?

The third reason is interesting because it is both difficult for some people to do in real life and because it is an opportunity that most designers ignore: know when you *don't* need permission!

Say you have two or more ways of designing something and they are fairly equal in terms of costs—they take the same amount of time, have the same chance of working, and they require the same resources to build. But what if one of them is a little more interesting? Or it will teach you something new? What if one is just a little cooler?

If there is no cost, or no extra cost, just pick one. You don't need to ask someone for permission to choose.

Similarly, as a designer, you are the expert. Doctors don't ask you what you think of their diagnosis; they *tell* you what it probably is. Be the expert! You don't have to ask permission for every little choice if you have good reasons for believing they are correct.

"Choose the Hill You Want to Die On"

There are a handful of expressions that I like as advice in real life, and although this is a cliché, it is one worth repeating (even to myself!). Not all fights are worth fighting.

Something I have learned far too slowly in my career is that it is often worth compromising or just giving a stakeholder something they want if it is not a key element of the user value of business value.

For example, copywriting is often something not worth fighting about. Copy is important, especially on critical buttons and headlines, but if you say no to the button copy the CEO wants, will she say no to the big important feature you need five developers to build?

There are many things you *can* fight about. You might even win! But there are only a few things *worth* fighting about. Avoid the small fights, be generous with choices that don't make a big difference, and *defend yourself* when it really matters!

But *when* it matters depends on where you work. So, let's get into that!

Working in Different Companies

UX at Startups

Here, I am not talking about big, famous tech companies; those aren't startups anymore. I mean companies that are smaller than a couple hundred people, funded by investors, and expected to grow as fast as they can.

Startups are short on time because they are growing faster than they can afford (or want to). This means they are literally *running out of money at all times!* And the only way to solve it is to grow their users or revenue fast enough to get more investments.

When resources are very tight and expectations are very high, you need to be a value machine. The smaller the company, the more you should focus on pure value creation. As it starts to work, you should live more and more in diagnosis mode. Generally, you don't have time for a lot of probability work until the company becomes more stable.

Be *ruthless* about your own time because you need every hour of work to take you closer to more value. If you're fine-tuning, you're wasting time. Time is everything at a startup!

UX at Big Companies

Honestly, enterprise UX sometimes makes me sad. At the very least, it often makes me bored, because I was raised in the fires of startups; but if big companies have one advantage over startups, it is *time*.

Anybody working in a big company and reading this might be tempted to tell me how busy they are and how much pressure there is to deliver. Yeah, but that is not pressure *caused* by a lack of time. It's caused by the complexity of the organization.

Big companies are big! It's a lot of people, and each of those people is far more specialized than in smaller companies. It takes a lot of processes, communications, and project management to make that work, which means people in big companies are literally doing *more work and more talking* to deliver the same project than they would in a smaller company.

A CEO I know once estimated that after a team becomes bigger than 16 people, they will spend more time organizing themselves than doing the actual work. At big companies you might work in teams of *hundreds* of people!

Smaller companies work simpler and faster. Big companies are more complex and slower. Your role in smaller companies will be to cover more of the work by yourself, and your role in big companies will be more focused on a specific part of the work.

In bigger companies, the difficult parts of UX are not related to the design itself, and frankly, they are not about VDP either! It's all about communication, how your team works together, and how well you can manage stakeholders. You will *feel* much further from the business model, but don't let that stop you.

You can often turn the VDP perspective on yourself and your team! How do you create value? Where are the problems in your processes and communication that you can solve? How can you improve the chances of delivering on time? Or getting approval from a stakeholder?

Quite often, when you have big company problems, it is because you see the work environment as something that happens to you instead of something you can *design*.

UX as a Team of One

If we're talking about big and small companies, it is worth touching on the idea of big and small *teams*. You can be the only UXer in a big company, and even small companies can have a big design team.

The smallest possible UX team (if it exists) is one designer. Just you!

The best thing and the worst thing about being a one-person army is that you control *everything* yourself! You have all the authority and all the responsibility. Every victory and every failure is you.

No, I lied. The best thing about being a one-person team is that you almost don't need documentation at all! A few notes about important choices might be enough. You will do more design and learn more as a designer when you work alone, but you will also work much, much harder than you would with a team, and you have to be more focused and more self-aware, all the time.

Prioritize carefully: keep scopes small, and do one (very valuable) thing at a time!

UX in a Big Team

We have discussed working with other UX designers and working in a big company already, so let me give you a more nuanced suggestion when you're working in a large team with many different roles, like a big product team: be known for something.

Regardless of who you are, there are often some parts of the work that you like more than others. Maybe you love analytics or you love user research or stakeholder meetings make your heart skip a beat (weirdo). Whatever it is, make sure your whole team knows that's your thing! (And if you're young, your thing can be trying new things!)

In a big team, you need a voice. Everybody should know who you are. At one job, I was called "the designer who measures everything," and therefore everything related to A/B testing always floated toward me. I loved it! In a team where nobody had feelings about analytics and A/B testing, that work would have been shared by several people, and maybe not done as well.

UX at Regulated Companies

Regulations can be different things. Banks are regulated, for example, but so are companies that sell to children online, and now every company that handles user data must be aware of privacy regulations. At any company that must comply with government regulations, designers are sometimes able to make very, very expensive mistakes.

When you join a regulated company, make the regulations an important item on your first to-do list. They are basically constraints for every project you will ever do there, and even though they are probably boring, you should become an expert as soon as possible.

I usually take an even more aggressive approach: treat regulations as a challenge. See *how well* you can comply with them. See *how well* you can know them, so everybody looks to you for answers.

Be *proud* of designing good solutions that also comply with regulations! Anybody can design something nice when there are no rules; only skilled designers can do it with regulations in the mix.

UX at Public Companies

One form of regulation is the rules that all companies on the stock market—*public* companies—must follow. I am not an expert in those rules, so I won't swim into the deep end here, but as a person working at one of those companies, you will have new and exciting reasons to create documentation and manage information about what you're working on.

In public companies, you might need to create enough documentation so an outsider can *trace* a decision back to its origin. So, if you design a button that accidentally deletes the bank accounts of everyone in the US, you should be able to show that it was the developer's fault, not yours. Traceability is just part of the rules!

You also need to manage information more carefully. There could be thousands or millions of people out there waiting for any little piece of information that helps them make money, and if you accidentally provide that information to a small group of people (i.e., not the *public*), that's bad. Like, jail-time bad.

Keep secrets. Respect security. Document well.

UX for a Famous Brand

Let's end this section on a fun topic: fame and creative opportunities! And also rules. Boo.

In my third year of professional design, I got my first job at a good agency and worked with a famous brand for the first time. I thought I was being creative when I designed a website that looked "much better" than their current site... Based on the amount of yelling that happened, I think my boss disagreed.

I made a rookie mistake: I didn't respect the brand guidelines. This is an issue that happens more and more in the digital world of fast-moving tech companies.

Companies like Coca-Cola or Volvo or Apple have enormous networks of user experiences, from stores to websites to billboards to coffee mugs in the gift shop. If every designer did something a little different, it would be hard to say what those companies look like, and the visual branding would fail.

In reality, we know exactly what they look like because famous brands have *rules*. And you should follow them! Like government regulations, a truly skilled designer will see them as a challenge, not a problem.

Famous brands, ironically, will also offer you some of the most exciting opportunities to do big, creative projects that push boundaries or gain exposure to millions or billions of people! Your job is not to question the brand rules, but to *interpret* them in creative ways that stay *consistent* with customer perceptions and expectations.

It's not easy, but it's very fun!

Whether it's a famous fashion brand or a highly regulated pharmaceutical company or a company traded on the stock market—or all three!—you should always start by gathering requirements and constraints and see them as input for your designs.

The greatest designers are able to take all the requirements and constraints, understand the user value and business value, follow a VDP-style process, and *still* produce amazing, creative, original, and inspiring products and services.

That's the job!

Quick Detour: Documents

Why I Haven't Focused on Documents in This Book

You may have noticed that there has been almost nothing about how to draw wireframes or make clickable prototypes or PowerPoint presentations or site maps or customer journey maps or any of that stuff. Do I really expect you to take this book as a guide for doing valuable UX in real companies without any documents?!

Yeah, kind of.

I am not saying you don't need to make documents. You will make plenty of them. But you can also search online about how to make most UX documents in 30 minutes or less. There is no "right way" to draw a customer journey map.

However, the *content* of those documents is highly important! And that has been the subject of most of this book. The rest of this book is all about *who* you are making documents for. The *content* and the *audience* of your documentation—regardless of what form or style it might take—is what matters.

Personally, I see documents as a form of *internal communication,* not design work.

Everybody Focuses on Documents!

Another reason I haven't gone all in on documentation is because *everybody else* teaches documents when they teach UX. UX documents are so easy to learn and teach that even the laziest of UX teachers will spend lots of time teaching documentation. Then they skip everything important.

UX documents feel important because they are the part that all of your colleagues will see. And in a way, that *does* make them very important. But remember: documents are only as valuable as the user value or the business value they communicate.

In reality, your skill as a document maker is the least important—but most *visible*—part of your job. Prioritize it accordingly. If you're presenting a year of research, make your documentation amazing! If you're just summarizing notes so they can collect dust in a SharePoint folder forever, maybe a quick-and-dirty text document is enough.

Hopefully you agree by now: there is more to UX than documents. Much, much more.

Some Quick Notes About Communicating with Documents

In my opinion, far too much design documentation is created in real companies. And the bigger the company, the worse it is. Most documents are never viewed or might be viewed once or twice. Only a handful of documents are really important, and those are often the ones nobody makes.

A good document is something you make well and something you use to unite a team and align the work of many people. A customer journey map or storyboard that you put on the wall and collaborate on with your colleagues is valuable. Do that and do it well.

Choose the level of detail and emphasize things based on what your *audience* needs to see and hear and learn. It makes me a little itchy when someone talks about UX documents out of context because it implies that your job is to deliver documentation. It's not. Your job is to create user value and business value.

Document that *value.*

Speaking of your colleagues, let's talk about some of them...

Working with Different Stakeholders

Everybody Can't Do UX

During the peak of UX fever, it became popular to say UX is just common sense. "Everybody can do UX!" It almost became taboo to suggest that UX designers know something other people don't.

By now, this book has shown you that UX is a set of *skills*. Skills require practice. There are principles and methods behind UX. While anybody *can learn* to do UX, most haven't. Everybody can't do UX any more than everybody can ride a unicycle.

When you add more people to decision making, the decisions get worse unless there are very high standards for educating those people. If you do user research with the wrong users, you will get feedback that you can't use. In a similar way, if you gather a bunch of colleagues together who are not good examples of your users, they cannot tell you what users think and feel.

And that does not make you superior to anyone! *You* can do UX. Your colleagues can also do things you can't. *Work together!*

The Benefits and Conflicts of Working Together

There are pros and cons to every colleague you have. As people, they are all valuable and interesting, of course, and many will be your friends, but over the next few sections we will (very briefly) discuss what you can learn from them or how they can help you design better solutions, and also how they will get in your way and make you want to run away and join the circus.

It is true that diverse teams and many perspectives create better solutions. Not because there are more people involved (see previous section), but because it gives you a more holistic understanding of a situation or a problem. Deeper understanding leads to deeper insights and smarter solutions.

Colleagues may also hold valuable information that you can't get or learn or access by yourself. They have often spent time in school studying things you have never heard of or years doing work you can't do or have lived in situations you haven't.

That's amazing! Use it!

UX Versus Sales

Salespeople are usually pretty great in terms of personalities. Not to put them all in one basket, but they persuade people all day for a reason. Technical salespeople or "solution architects" can also be a nice bridge between you and developers and other salespeople.

For the purposes of creating *value*, it is good to realize that salespeople talk with potential customers all day and hear both yes and no a lot. As a UX designer looking for insights and feedback, both of those answers are useful.

Knowing what hooks a lot of new customers is great because it either confirms you are creating value or shows you where to create more. Knowing what customers *don't* like also tells you what to fix or stay away from.

But be careful...Salespeople also love to ask what you're cooking up in the design team. And if you tell them too soon, you might hear them selling it to a real customer long before they should! Also, remember that they might ask for things they want to sell, too, even if real customers don't value those ideas as much.

Listen to salespeople! Then verify.

If Sales is a key stakeholder for your work, then you should frame your conversation in terms of how it helps them close deals or increase the average deal value. Any discussion that is focused on the craft or philosophy of design might be lost on a sales audience because it is very hard to see how that connects with deals or customers. Happy or excited customers are more likely to buy, and that should relate to *something* you do!

But frankly, if you can't connect your design with deals in a company with a sales team...you're missing something.

UX Versus Marketing

In the real world, designers of all kinds can be on the marketing team, including UX. *Very often* it is a bad sign when the head of Marketing manages UX designers, because it means management might not realize the value of UX design beyond *communications*. Generally speaking, UX should be on the Product or Design team, but every company can be unique that way.

We have already looked at the difference between *marketing-driven* UX and *revenue-driven* UX, so let's talk about marketers! They might be doing advertising or communication strategy or creative work or search engine optimization (SEO) or conversion optimization with more of a campaign focus. In fact, you both might use the same user analytics but with different priorities!

Product (including UX) and Marketing should work closely together in most companies. In B2C companies, marketing will own the brand, and UX must support the brand experience. In B2B companies, marketing will work more closely to sales. In all companies, Product must deliver what Marketing promises, and vice versa.

Share information! Look for overlapping insights. Be two links in the same chain. You have the power to make their work *convert better*, and they can send you more and better users to convert. Their branding will add creative and emotional value to your efficient, functional interfaces. And your products and services will be exposed to more people and have more influence because marketers are doing their job.

For that reason, discussions with marketing people should usually focus on this intersection between function and communications. When aligned, it can be a very potent combination.

UX Versus Product

We will talk about developers soon, and we just said UX is ideally *part* of the Product team. So, here we're talking about product managers, product owners, and roles like that.

If you're lucky, your product manager or product owner will have a background as a designer or developer, and they will understand what is involved when "doing" rather than just "managing." But if they don't, the risk is that your work will be seen as isolated *tasks* or *productivity* rather than problem-solving work that takes time to figure out along the way.

It can be good to talk to product managers about how you like to work and what is required, so they understand the work itself a little better. But in the same way, you should talk to them about the strategy, the bigger priorities on the product road map, and how your work fits into the big picture. That's their job!

When good designers and good product managers come together, the result is a lot of very smart trade-offs. They will provide a better strategic view of your work and help you prioritize, and you will provide a better detailed view of the work, helping them understand the real-world process of bringing the planned product to life.

Within the product team, the UX person might have to fight for *research*. When creating *value* for the first time or *diagnosing* a problem that you don't understand yet, speak to the product manager about the effects on the road map and the success of the product as a whole if the value isn't created or the problem isn't solved.

I once found data in a company's analytics that showed 90% of users dropped off after the second step of a registration flow, but without an obvious reason. Without a cause, they almost ignored it, until I explained to the product manager that all future product work and marketing campaigns would be worth 90% less unless we solved that issue. A month later, it was fixed (the problem was in the database!).

UX Versus Key Performance Indicators (KPIs)

OK, OK, I know what you're thinking: KPIs aren't colleagues. And you're right, of course. But KPIs are decided by colleagues and not always for reasons that have any relationship to reality.

I chose to mention this here because the Product Managers we just discussed usually love KPIs. And there is nothing wrong with that. KPIs, when used properly, are just good ways to measure your solutions. All good designers will measure their solutions to learn and improve.

So, what's the problem?

KPIs have a way of trying to predict what "good" looks like in the future. Like saying the goal is a 20% improvement in conversion before any research work begins. Is 20% good? Is 20% possible? Do we have any idea how to make that happen yet?

My standard joke is, "Should I stop when I get to 20%?"

KPIs are the *metrics* you should measure. Not the *amount* of improvement you desire.

UX Versus Developers

I laugh every time a UX designer is annoyed with a developer. It's a love/hate relationship to be sure, and often it combines the people who have the highest need for accurate, logical communication (devs) with the people who have the highest need for conceptual, emotional solutions (designers).

It is precisely that difference (again, stereotyping!) that makes a good developer/designer pair so valuable in real life. Designers can turn abstract, irrational problems and highly unreliable stakeholder input into a specified solution that is precise and well supported. And developers can take a theoretical drawing of a solution and make it into a fully functional product that didn't exist or work yesterday.

It's beautiful when you think about it!

Good developers will make you a better thinker and a more pragmatic designer. But be careful, not all developers (or designers) are good. Lazy developers might talk you out of good ideas because they are hard to build or take shortcuts you don't want.

That being said, developers are great. Find a good one and sit beside them.

Why Coders Love "Agile" and UX Designers Don't

Imagine you have noticed a pattern in your user data, and you have a feeling (but no evidence) that there is a problem with a form on your website. But you have no idea what that problem might be.

How long will it take you to find the problem? And before you find it, how long will it take to solve?

If you have no idea, you're not alone. That's what a lot of real design work looks like, and unfortunately, a lot of "agile" ways of working like Scrum assume that the size of a task can be estimated in advance.

On the other hand, after the designer has identified the problem and defined the solution, a developer has a pretty good idea of the scope. Estimating the time needed for that is a reasonable request. Agile for the win.

Some design tasks are easy to estimate, and some coding tasks are abstract, too, but the balance is quite different, which makes agile a better fit for coding and a worse fit for UX.

UX Versus Customer Support

Usually, or at least anywhere I have ever worked, UX and Support are very different teams. Sometimes they are literally on opposite sides of the building. But they are a pair of roles that go together like chocolate and strawberries.

Customer support people usually don't get a lot of authority and spend all day listening to people complain, be confused, or generally be unhappy about the product or service experience. It's not a glamorous job, and that is exactly why they will love you.

UX people often forget about the Support team, but you will love them just as much, I promise! All of those negative things they deal with are extremely valuable information for you. They can tell you some of the most valuable problems to solve, and they want to tell you *really badly*!

Go talk to a Support person who has worked at the company for a long time. It will be worth your time, every time.

UX Versus UX

Is this déja vu? Nope, it's just a big UX team. In large companies it is common to have lots of UX people with more specialized roles. UX copywriters, UX researchers, UX designers, people who maintain the design system, people who do the UI, and I am sure somewhere there is a UX coffee manager or similar.

As a one-person team, which is common, you must/can do a lot of different things. But when a person with that experience suddenly must coordinate with another UXer, sometimes it feels like you get less authority. Don't think of it like that. Think of it as more *depth* in whatever area you focus on.

Other UXers will understand your work like nobody else, so don't compete. Actively split up the work so everybody gets a piece. If everyone does their job properly, the results should be better overall.

Like all collaborations, working with other UX designers just means more communication (documents!) along the way. Agree on how to communicate before you start, not after you are frustrated.

UX Versus UI

This is my favorite way to work in UX—together with a UI designer. A good UI designer will understand, or at least appreciate, why UX exists, but their priorities will be all about the look and feel of the final interface. In this case, UX should lean into structure and functionality so UI can really shine in the visuals and interaction details.

Personally, I believe this combination is the best of both worlds. But since there is overlap in the middle, it can be a little tricky to separate who gets to decide what.

The layout of a page, for example, might look one way in your wireframes, and then the UI might try to move things in a significant way, which ruins some of the visual probabilities you had created. In that case, you just have to discuss it and explain.

On the other hand, I often look for *opportunities* to *not* decide something if that will allow the UI designer to look at it in detail. Don't fight for authority; *leave space* for each other!

UX Versus Project Managers

Project managers (PMs) are an influential piece of any team. They often think they are much more influential than they are, but whether they are good or bad at their job, you will feel it. Good project managers are worth their weight in gold, and bad project managers can make it impossible to work at all.

The key to working well with your project managers is to understand how *they* decide what is important, and to stand up for your needs when it really matters, as early as possible.

PMs are usually concerned with time, budget, and the client or stakeholders. At an agency, the client might be an external company with their own PM. Help PMs understand your process and how different plans will affect time and budget.

Time and budget (i.e., costs) are usually not the best ways to measure design quality or user value, and clients/stakeholders usually have other priorities that might not even be rational. ("My daughter likes blue; make it blue.")

That means the PM and the client or stakeholders might ask for something too big or to be done too fast or change the expectations of the project. Tell them! Often you can only *recommend* what should be done, and you must follow orders if they disagree, but still tell them.

And with PMs, the most critical phase of a project might be the beginning when everyone is estimating the time or budget needed to complete the work. Always assume that your work will take 10–30% longer than you think, and if the budget is fixed, reduce the amount of work (the scope) until you are confident you can finish without going over.

That "padding" is a good professional habit, but that isn't the only reason to do it. Eventually a PM will prioritize the client's or the stakeholder's wishes over you and your realistic expectations, and you will *need* that extra time to make everything blue!

If you finish early or under budget, they'll be happy. The opposite, not so much.

UX Versus Finance

During your early days of design, you may not have a lot of reason to think about anything financial, but as you rise up the ladder you will influence budgets, lead projects, and maybe even propose what work should be done.

If you can decide what work should be done, eventually you will be in a meeting with someone who is responsible for the money—finance people.

I like to think of Finance as Google Analytics for a whole company. It's all the numbers about where all the money goes and what everything costs, without any of the details that say why or how those numbers happen.

So, when you have meetings with financial folks, you have two simple tasks: tell them about the money, and tell them what the money means for the company.

If your project will reduce costs or increase profits or sell more or allow you to support more customers, that's good. Tell them, and use numbers or data to tell them. That's the first part.

In the words of investors, you should also "add color" to the numbers. Sometimes design will increase profit by increasing the conversion rate, which means you're making more money by adding efficiency to something you already do. If you can add 10% more revenue for a one-time cost of A/B testing for two months, that's probably a good deal!

The "analytics" perspective might give finance people limited insight into the nuts and bolts of what you do—which can be frustrating in its own way—but it also gives them an overview of the company you might never have.

Remember, one of the ways you can add value with design is to *reduce costs*. Nobody knows the costs better than the finance department!

Help them connect the dots on a design level, and they can help you do the same on the business level.

UX Versus Leadership

If Product and Finance need more "big picture" thinking from you, then the C-suite (the CEO, COO, CFO, CMO, etc.) requires the biggest picture. They manage the whole company, and from that high up, design work is just machinery making the business strategy work.

But that doesn't mean your work isn't important! Senior management like the C-suite, and any other higher-ups, spend so much of their time thinking about how to achieve the goals of the company and beat competition and where to go in the future, they just don't have the same context as a typical designer.

In that way, this book can really help you have those conversations.

But if there is any room where "design for its own sake" will die an awkward, silent death, it is with senior management. I have seen some pretty rough presentations where designers go into the details of their design techniques with a CEO, and they leave the meeting with a no, or worse—no respect.

It can be hard to speak the language of senior management, but when you get the chance, you should try. How will the design work create or grow the company's competitive advantages? How does it support long-term goals and big strategies like the ecosystem, or how does it help acquire new, bigger, or better customers?

In short: don't worry about your design choices; just focus on how they help *the whole company.*

Working with Users

User Research in Real Life

When students get into a real job after learning UX in a boot camp or university or some other not-really-doing-real-design type of education, they are often surprised to find out that user research is hard to do, or hard to get *permission* to do in real life.

If this happened to you, and you thought to yourself, "How do I know what to design if we don't talk to users?"—you are absolutely correct! Unfortunately, that might not help you do real user research at your real job.

First, I think it is worth giving you a less *grand* idea of what user research must look like. If you *can* do super professional studies in a usability lab with eye tracking and carefully designed studies (like academics might do), that is great—do it! But if you are in the other 99% of companies, you can get a *lot* of valuable information from a much-less-formal study of users.

My favorite starting point is one-on-one interviews, maybe with a casual task or two in your product or website, and some fairly open, simple questions that I ask everyone. Five users, no gift cards or any other payments, and the users are selected based on a few important but simple criteria to make sure they are the right kind of people (real users are not all exactly the same, and in reality only a handful of factors make them relevant...don't filter for more than that; otherwise you risk creating a bias toward the answers you *want*!).

Watch those users in real time, record everything that happens, and after you do 5–10 of those, go back through them to find clusters of behavior and insights.

When user testing is free and fast and you know *why* you are doing it and the users aren't super painful to find—which is most user testing—and you have no concerns about being a public company or anything...there is no reason to say no to user testing. In a lot of companies, you might not even *need* to ask permission to formally plan that work. Just go get some relevant testers and do it! All the time! One user per week adds up to many great insights over several months or a year.

In real life, user testing is very, very valuable, and very, very few companies do it as a routine or an active search for information. Sometimes the UX people are just lazy (don't be one of those) or intimidated (try it, it's easy!) or they get stuck on problems like "I don't have a budget for testing!" which might not even matter to the real testers. Lots of people think it is fun to test and give input; just ask!

For me, user testing is a reflex. I start talking about it right away in a project, I do it spontaneously, and I do it even if the quality of the testing isn't as controlled and well designed as I would like it to be. Talking to real people about using something is valuable all by itself!

There is almost never a good excuse for not doing user research, unless there are no real users (your *colleagues or AI chat tools are NOT substitutes for real, relevant users!!!*) or there is a government regulation or security risk preventing you from exposing users to a work-in-progress. But I have done user research in all those scenarios, so it really is an extreme case when user testing is just impossible.

Worst case, be a user *observer*. Watch people on the bus or in the office as they work, test competitor products to see weaknesses you can learn from, or start working on a small testing budget now so you can do testing later.

If you have never seen real people using what you're designing or talked to real users about using something like that, you have a *huge* gap in your knowledge. As a designer, and as a company. And that gap can kill you.

Your Biggest Results Will Come from Good Research

You cannot generate true innovation in a meeting with your colleagues. Workshops, brainstorming sessions, and other meetings with your colleagues are just meetings in different clothing. If you don't include real users in your design process, you are absolutely missing all of the best ideas.

After 20+ years of designing products and services, almost 100% of my best real-world results have come from research insights. Although it happens, it is very rare to get one of those lightning-strike ideas out of nowhere.

Research, including user research, is the most reliable way to generate great ideas (i.e., great solutions). Ask good questions, listen carefully, and then think about what you heard. Discuss it with your team if you can too!

Starting with research ensures that you are only looking at real problems. Not theoretical or hypothetical problems, not small problems that nobody actually has, and not problems that users consider details.

Your biggest results will come from research. Start there, every time.

I Often Start with Data, Not Users

Throughout this book, we have talked about two broad categories of research: users and data. User research is critical and valuable, but it is not necessarily the first thing you should do. I always start with data if I can. There are two reasons for that.

The first reason is that users are humans, and humans do odd things like lying or telling you parts of the answer and hiding the rest because it is embarrassing, or giving different opinions depending on their mood or how much they like you personally during the test.

If you *start* with subjective, unreliable opinions, you need to do a lot more *interpreting* during the next steps of your research, and everything takes longer.

The second reason to start with data is that it is easy to access. If you are collecting analytics, all you have to do is long in, and voila! There it is. You don't need permission or other people or any logistics of booking times for testing or any of that. And you can check your data every week if you want!

Start with data and look for patterns, or exceptions, that might be meaningful. Pages that get much more or much less traffic or that people use for longer. Flows (i.e., funnels) where one step is much worse than the others. Days that generated a lot more traffic or much worse behavior suddenly, especially if the trend went back to normal immediately after. And so on.

Those data patterns focus you on something specific. *Then* go get some users, and specifically test *whatever is creating the data pattern*. Sometimes you can go look at that part of the product and immediately see a potential cause of the data pattern; then you just need to verify it, which is quick research work.

The goal of all research is to have several clues that all point to one hypothesis. Data and users are two separate sources of information. When they seem to agree, there is a good chance you are right. But data is faster, so start there.

Why Complicated Methods Are Usually Worse

Simple methods can make people feel unsophisticated. Marketers (or consultants with a framework to sell) *want* you to feel unsophisticated. They want to sell something more complicated! Analytics tools began as plain data in tables and charts, and they are becoming sophisticated AI-assistants and automated reports that actually do *less* than the plain-data version, and this is why.

As I have mentioned, your best insights will probably come from simple questions and good listening skills. That's it! Your best data insights will come from the simple kind of theory in this book: Where are the valuable problems, the related symptoms, and the probabilities? Then you simply have to understand the big picture of your company to see how these insights fit. That is all UX work, all the time, forever.

Very detailed, small areas of optimization, like one blue color or another blue color are almost always a waste of time. The exception is products with billions of users, like Google, where even a tiny optimization can be worth millions more in revenue (but that kind of work is highly statistical, not just general user testing).

When you start to focus on minute details for more than a few minutes, there is a risk that you are bike-shedding. What is bike-shedding? Good question with a funny answer.

In 1957, a group of scientists studied a planning committee that was designing a nuclear power plant. In all of that complex, technical, and highly regulated work, the topic they discussed most was...wait for it...the employee bike shed. From a VDP context, that would not even be on the map, and yet, it got a lot of attention!

Humans like discussing details because they are concrete, but most details are trivial or worthless in the big picture. Complicated research methods and highly detailed methods of prioritizing or designing almost always give the trivial details too much attention, while the big picture suffers.

VDP! Create value, diagnose the most valuable problems, and then optimize until there is something more valuable to do.

The Exception: High Volumes of Users

It is worth expanding on this idea of millions or billions of users and how that should affect you as the researcher. Really, it is a question of probabilities.

As a general principle, something that affects 60% of users is more valuable than something that affects 20% of users. But as you work through those big problems, the *percentage* of affected users gets smaller quickly. A handful of problems will affect users in general, and the rest will affect smaller and smaller groups of users.

If we're talking *percentages*. If we're talking absolute *number* of users, though, a small percentage might still be a lot of people!

When you have 10,000 users, a problem that affects 1 out of 10,000 people is probably not worth solving unless it launches a deadly virus into the atmosphere or something. But if you have a billion users, that tiny percentage is still 100,000 people!

At that scale you will certainly be able to work with a data scientist or similar specialist to analyze the data, and you should, because those problems are hard to see as an individual designer or when interviewing individual users. You would need to interview thousands of people just to see that problem once! Maybe!

The fewer users you have, the more you should lean on individual user research and spend time with real, individual humans, because your data is worse and the problems you're solving are bigger and more common. But the more users you have, the more you should lean on data and statistical analysis to solve problems.

To do statistical research, you also need to control your studies more carefully because little differences in the questions you ask or the *way* you collect data can have a big influence when multiplied by a billion users. Generally, we're talking about a UX lab or fine-tuned data analysis.

Although this might seem like a luxurious problem to have, you should always consider the *probabilistic* view of how you do research. Even the difference between 10 and 1,000 users can shift your methods.

Accessibility

Sometimes there is a bit of confusion between *accessibility* and *usability*. And sometimes that makes designers ignorant, so let's clear that up first.

Although these two things are definitely related—different points on the same spectrum of difficulty, you might say—generally, *usability* assumes that the user is fully functional as a person and *able* to use your design in a fundamental way. An informal definition, to be sure, but still. Accessibility doesn't assume those things. Although it certainly includes dramatic disabilities like blindness and deafness, we can also include people who need strong reading glasses, like older people, or color-blind people (10% of the male population). And we can go even further and talk about people with old phones or unreliable internet connections or low incomes (data is expensive in many countries!) or no email addresses or those who don't speak the language very well. Some companies are successful just by offering a common product, translated for immigrants. Brilliant!

Usability is about how *well* an average user can use your design. Accessibility is about the *required capabilities* to use your design. On the scale of a million people, like any public service in any major city, accessibility is a necessity, not a luxury.

But now that we have that sorted out a little bit, I want to provoke you to stop *asking* for accessibility. Either do it without asking or *fight* for it.

For a small company or a niche product or a low budget, do accessibility *secretly*. Good design should be fairly accessible anyway. Don't talk about special accessibility work, just build it into everything you design, all the time. Ensure that your text is readable with the screen light on a low setting, make sure it still makes sense for users who can't see the color of the buttons, and make sure it works well enough on all relevant devices and "fails gracefully" when it doesn't work as well.

When accessibility is *necessary*, fight for it. Remember: good designers welcome more constraints! A subway system website, for example, serves a broad section of society and is not complete without accessibility.

Not sure how? See *https://www.a11yproject.com*.

Protip: Make Users Comfortable First

It is easy to be so focused on what *we* want from a user test that we forget to think about the user's experience of the *test itself.*

Even when testers think it is fun, they can be nervous or self-conscious or worried about making mistakes. Ironically, we *want* them to make mistakes so we can see it, but that doesn't stop the testers from having those feelings.

Explain that you are not testing *them.* *They* are testing the product. You are just there to record the results. I offer to keep testers anonymous if they want so they can be more honest. And then I don't share their face or name internally! If you are not the designer of the product being tested (or even if you are), you can say, "Don't worry about hurting my feelings, I didn't design this!" or "My job is to find problems, so if you find something confusing or difficult, that's great!"

Take away the fear of failure for the tester! You'll get better results.

Observation

The simplest of user research techniques. Free, natural, and usually pretty easy to do. Highly recommended!

If you truly feel like you're in the dark about what to research or how to start doing research at your company, just invite a few users to use your product as you watch. No rules, no tasks, no formal questions. Just watch. As long as you can.

Quite quickly, you will see someone do something in the wrong order. Or in a sequence you had not expected. Or combine features in a way they were not designed to be used. None of that is wrong!

It's *interesting*.

Ask why! Ask what they were trying to do. Maybe show them another way to do it and talk about why they didn't do that already. Just observe and be curious!

Observation can also be done outside of work when you're lucky enough to see people using your product "in the wild." Don't interrupt! Just watch, like David Attenborough watching animals in their natural habitat.

Surveys

I have a love/hate relationship with surveys. I have seen several studies that say a typical market research-style survey can be wrong by up to 30%. I have personally done surveys where some of the questions were objectively true or false, and in fact, the results were up to 40% wrong! And that's when the question *isn't* open to interpretation!

In general, surveys are something I avoid, except in two cases: specific questions for a large population and when it is hard to access *anybody* for some reason.

If you need to understand the shifting opinions of a large population of people or companies, then a survey might be the only true way to do that. That quickly becomes statistical research, and the same principles we have already discussed apply.

If you need to ask 50 CEOs some questions, it can be very hard to book meetings with that type of people (for example), but they are often willing to answer a quick survey instead. That doesn't give you *statistical* answers to your questions—be careful about how you analyze them!—but it does give you answers.

Surveying small groups of people makes your "data" highly unreliable, but as a smart human, you know that, and you can avoid making detailed, high-cost decisions based *only* on that data. And sometimes a survey is great to *verify* that a certain opinion is consistent with your data-based hypothesis. Maybe your internal data indicates that CEOs love turkey sandwiches, and you just need a feeling about whether that hypothesis is true.

During college I spent three years verbally asking people surveys as my part-time job. I can tell you firsthand, even the most well-designed survey will not deliver exactly perfect results. But even on the phone, 50 or 100 people quickly give you a sense of what a general trend might look like.

With surveys, go big or use them as support and nothing more. Never fully trust the results of surveying a small number of people, and any broader interpretation of survey results should be checked for assumptions.

User Tasks

I want to be a little bit careful with the topic of user tasks, because my priority in this book is to give you real-world, pragmatic advice that helps you take shortcuts when it is an advantage and avoid shortcuts when it will hurt you.

Quantitative measurements of user tasks are not always a valuable thing to measure. Something like the time it takes for users to go from A to B success-fully requires a lot of data to be accurate, and in reality users will go from A to B for a lot of different reasons.

So, should I recommend user tasks for the sake of learning those reasons, or should I not recommend user tasks because they don't provide meaningful data unless you do large-scale testing?

Both! User tasks must be *designed* for the context you are testing. And you know what? Almost *nobody* does that. You should! You must! Design each and every user test so it answers the questions you have; don't expect a random task to magically provide insights that are useful!

User Interviews

Unlike surveys and user tasks, I almost always find it valuable to *interview* users. Tasks become a much more insightful form of testing when you follow the task with a good interview that digs into whatever happened in the task.

And the best interviews are almost always simple interviews. The key to good interviews is not complexity; it's how *structured* the interview is. For a smaller number of people (say, less than 100, which is almost every research project you will ever do), the best insights come from *semistructured* interviews. Have a list of questions, and choose them carefully, but be prepared to improvise and ask unique follow-up questions depending on what users say.

So, you start the same way and cover the same topics for every user, but you also leave room for things you didn't expect. Then *unpack those things*! When a user says something like, "Then I ask my dog, and go from there!" you should feel free to say, "Tell me more about your dog; how does he help you go from there?"

Listen for things you can *unpack*. Words that mean processes like "make" or complex feelings like "favorite" or decisions like "choose." Then unpack them, by asking users what they mean!

The more users you will interview in one project (or the more specific the answers must be), the more structured your interview should be. An interview done with a million people is technically a survey! At a large scale, every question should be exactly identical, and you should limit the answers so they can be counted more easily.

Small sets of interviews should be flexible, large sets of interviews should be strict.

Protip: ask questions that sound simple, but make people think. For example, I might ask something like, "How has this book changed your thinking about your work?"

Not a hard question to understand, but pretty hard to answer! Answers to a question like that create opportunities to ask deeper questions than lead to really valuable, nuanced insights.

Focus Groups (and Why They Suck)

One of the most shared quotes from *UX for Beginners* is, "I would rather light myself on fire than do a focus group." I stand by that.

In a focus group, you interview a bunch of users, as a group. Unlike interviews, a focus group creates *social dynamics*. Shy people become quiet, dominant people take over, strong opinions start to be accepted by more people, and unique opinions get lost. Embarrassing or "weird" experiences are not shared, and the whole group starts to become one big, dumb version of the loudest person.

Unless your deadline is tomorrow, individual interviews would get you deeper answers, more answers, and less bias. Focus groups are rarely the best choice.

But there is one big exception! When you need a group (like stakeholders) to understand *negative* situations, group discussions can be amazing.

The first example is when you *want* the group to form a new opinion. Imagine a team of colleagues who don't prioritize usability because they don't experience it personally (dogfooding prevents this!). It's hard to get *buy-in* from stakeholders who don't care about usability.

Put them all in one room and give them a usability task! And candy! Make it a race! Yay! As they all have the same, difficult experience, they will bond over their collective failure, and that project will magically jump to the top of the priority list! Group task for the win.

Another example is when a group is underperforming. Most people are insulted if you tell them, individually, that they are doing something wrong. But a *group* creates a feeling of safety because you're not pointing at any one person. Instead of telling Jim that he doesn't know who the target user is, put Jim in a group and ask the whole group, "Who is the target user?" When nobody has a good answer, Jim will feel like he is not alone, but you will also verify the problem in front of everyone. Then nobody will doubt why you want to fix it!

Don't Help Users

One of the best tips for user testing is to shut up during user testing.

After you have made them comfortable and set the stage, explained the tasks, and they have begun that task, don't talk. It's a little awkward sometimes, I won't lie, but shut up anyway! The last thing you say to users before they begin testing the product should be something like, "I am not allowed to help you, so take your time and do whatever you would do if I wasn't here." They won't, but still.

Whether you are asking structured questions and waiting for their answer, or watching them do a set task, every comment you make can change their perception of what they are doing. When you do need to ask a question, like, "Why did you choose to click that?" try very hard to keep your phrasing neutral. Don't ask a leading question like, "Did you click that because it was red and vibrating?" Quite often they will just say yes because you made one answer easier than anything else.

And when a user answers your questions, try to confirm in a neutral way, like "OK" or "I understand," rather than saying "That's great!" with enthusiasm or "Oh, that's not good" with sympathy. Why? Because then you are agreeing with them or telling them what is a "good" answer (or not). People are quick to pick up on those cues and might start giving you the answer they think you want, instead of the truth.

But the worst version of this—the worst!—is *helping* a user complete the task. The *moment* you say something like "Are you stuck? It's that button there..." you have just ruined the whole test. Now they know you will help if they hesitate, you have *trained* them about how to do the task in real time, and everything they do after your help is not realistic. In real life, they might have failed to complete the task, and now you will never know!

During a user test, act like every word you say costs money: shhhh!

Everybody Lies

Users are people. All people lie sometimes. Usually, our lies make other people feel better or protect us from feeling bad about something—nothing weird or unholy about that. But when your goal is to learn about the mistakes and negative feelings and problems that users experience, lying can be a real obstacle.

Making users feel comfortable at the beginning of a test is a good start (discussed earlier). In addition to that, you can also design your interviews and tasks in a way that minimizes the chance of something embarrassing happening, such as saying, "Type in an answer, but it doesn't have to be true."

Help testers feel like it's "you and them" against the product, instead of "you and the product" against the tester. Tell them you appreciate their time, tell them when they say something interesting or valuable, and help them understand that weird answers are helpful!

Don't *approve* their answers! Just be appreciative when they answer well. "That's interesting, tell me more about that."

User Testing with External Services

External user testing services are like the sirens of legend: they seduce you with their song of convenience and automation, and then they drown you in complexity and bias.

Good reasons to use external services include organizing your results in a structured way with video recordings, making results available to a larger team or stakeholders, ensuring that more junior UX people follow the plan, and finding test users that might otherwise be hard to get like people in smaller, faraway countries or less common languages.

The *risks* of using external services include *very* high costs compared to the simple user testing I recommend, being lazy with the design of your test and then repeating that laziness automatically, testing users who are *professional testers* and therefore biased, and being forced to select users based on criteria that are not what you care about.

Test automation or big testing software products do not make you better at user research. They just make the research easier *at a large scale*. Make sure that's why you're paying for it.

A/B Testing

...is a beautiful thing. Highly underrated! Although I have had many interesting conversations about the nuances of A/B testing with UXers, when done well, they are one of the best ways to make UX decisions or settle arguments. And some UX decisions are just unknowable unless you test them against each other!

Since we're in "The Who" section of the book, let's start with A/B testing as an argument-ender. It is very common for designers or stakeholders to think they can predict what a million people will prefer, even when there is no reason to think they can.

Test it! Design both options, make an A/B test, and *prove* who is right. Argument settled! If they *still* want to fight, run the test again! How many times can they be proven wrong and keep arguing?!

When trying to understand users, you may never be able to *decide* whether a million users prefer strawberry or raspberry ice cream more. Only an A/B test can tell you which subjective preference this particular group of users likes more.

A/B tests can be applied to different kinds of problems. Some of the results can be taken to all future projects too! And some will have to be repeated with every new group of users to verify.

A *structural* question, like optimizing the conversion of a flow or improving the flow of visitors to a particular feature, can often teach you something about humans in general (all the probabilistic thinking in this book is based on that kind of testing!).

But a *contextual* question like "strawberries or raspberries" is not a universal truth. Maybe strawberries win when you're selling ice cream and raspberries win when you're selling cheesecake. Who knows?!

A/B testing is a brilliant way to make decisions when the *human factor* of users is the main question of your research.

Working with Yourself

We Are Human

The humanity of our users, customers, stakeholders, and colleagues is a quiet theme through everything in UX, business, and this book. Really, when you think about it, all of those things are much more about how products work for humans than anything else. Imagine how easy this would all be if people were all the same, every time!

As humans, we all make mistakes. Including you and including me! But all mistakes are not created equal either. There are different flavors of "mistakes," and it is really helpful to learn to recognize the differences.

Sometimes we might do the wrong thing, not because it is incorrect or doesn't work, but because it moves the product or the company in the wrong *direction*. A feature that users *like* when you ask them might also cause them to *leave* our product or *cost* the business more without adding any value. It's not "wrong"...it's just not *right*.

Sometimes we might often give ourselves *rules* that nobody wants or needs, but since we think that is a rule, we will ignore certain solutions that would be smarter. For example, if you have spent too much time listening to design influencers and you think buttons must look a certain way all the time, you might miss an opportunity to make a *weird* button that isn't as trendy but will be seen by more users and convert better (as in, special buttons). Nobody gave you that rule, and it's not a requirement or constraint of the project, but you still followed that rule and did the "wrong" thing.

In this final section of the book, I will give you a few examples of times when *you*, the designer, are the source of the problem. It happens to all of us, and it's hard to see, but when it happens, only you can solve it.

How to Convince Stakeholders: Another Perspective

UX people, like most other kinds of people, think about ourselves more than anyone else. Notice that everybody asks, "How can I convince stakeholders?" and nobody asks, "How can I be more valuable to stakeholders?"

We don't do this on purpose, we just do it.

99% of the problem of convincing a stakeholder starts with the fact that we, the designers, create our processes, our decisions, and our documents with *our own priorities in mind*. A very ironic problem for people in a job that is entirely built around solving *other people's problems!*

If you reverse your perspective on all design work and all stakeholders, all the time, and consider it your job to deliver value to those stakeholders (including users!), then you will change the way you see your process, your decisions, and your documentation.

Stop serving yourself or "the design perspective." Stakeholders will respond positively.

The Right Thing Versus Your Favorite Thing

Junior designers fall in love with ideas. Senior designers fall in love with solutions. And that is not a subtle difference.

An idea is something that is *possible*. Ideas don't necessarily solve the problem well or meet the requirements or create value for the users and the business. However, they might look or sound really cool, and the designer might *really* want to design them!

A good *solution* will solve the problem, meet the requirements, and create value for everyone. They might not look or sound particularly cool, and often they might even be common and therefore boring.

A good solution is always the right thing to do. Whether that is your favorite idea is irrelevant.

Make Things Easier for Users, Not Yourself

A lot of design and business problems are hard to solve! Especially if you have tight deadlines and budgets and a lot of requirements to consider! In those situations, you might get tired of struggling with the problem. In those moments, you will be tempted to do something worse just to be "done," even if it doesn't solve the problem for the user.

Resist.

When you make a weak solution just to save time or effort, you are creating a trap for yourself. In a way, you are giving your *future self* more problems so your *current self* can have less problems. That's not good.

Often the best solutions are hard work for the designers and developers, but magically delicious for the users. Those are huge wins, waiting to happen! But when you are the designer or developer struggling with it, it's easy to forget that.

Users can't see whether it was hard or easy for you. They only care about whether it is hard or easy for them. Prioritize correctly!

Discovery Versus Research

I have worked with several companies where nobody, including the managers, have ever learned anything about user research. Their first step in the design process is to look at competitors to find ideas to copy. They call this "discovery."

That is not research.

When you do more creative design work, like UI styling or marketing design, a lot of that work is based on "inspiration," and it can be very helpful to look around for cool examples or new creative trends or clever details that other designers have made. Do it!

But UX doesn't work like that, especially for business. This whole book has described ways to make decisions based on the problems *you* have found at *your* company and with *your* users and *their* context! So, why would you go look for solutions based on *other* situations?

Copying competitors or designing based on inspiration ignores *both* user value and business value and prioritizes *your own* preferences instead.

And! What if the solution you're copying isn't working for the competitors either? Oops!

Research Theater Is Bad for Everyone

While writing this book, I had a real project that suffered from a problem I call *research theater*. It's when people pretend to do research, or even when they actually make time for research activities, but don't actually care about results.

One of the best ways to know if research is real or theater is to look at the plans for *after* research. Real research often generates bad news, and then you need more research or you will kill the idea and move on to something else. Real research sometimes tells you what *not* to do!

Research *theater* doesn't care about results. That's bad. Those people will plan more development or a launch campaign or some other commitment *based on the positive results* of the research—*before* the research happens. Either they are psychic or they are going to move ahead regardless of what testing says. That is research theater.

It hurts everyone because it teaches stakeholders, junior people on the team, and your own managers that research and testing don't matter. Research and testing really, really matter. They are the basis of VDP.

Treat Causes, Not Symptoms

The diagnostic process starts by looking for *clusters* of symptoms that might have a common cause. That means you can't start solving the problem when you find the first symptom; you must keep looking for more symptoms.

In real life, it is often tempting to jump into action as soon as you see the first problem instead of looking for the cause of that problem. You might want to design something to *hide* that symptom.

For example, if you see that your blog has a high bounce rate, you could add a start page with one button that takes you to a default page. Since that is so easy, the bounce rate for the site will get better, but have you really improved anything? Most users will leave on the next page instead, so you have really just *hidden* the symptom instead of finding the root cause. You should design a better start page instead.

If you had realized that the bounce rate only looked "high" because you were comparing it to a site with a different structure (like a search-oriented content site), then it might not even be a problem!

When you solve each symptom, one at a time, you start to create complexity, because the root cause of those symptoms still exists, but you are adding more and more details to hide all the symptoms. Users are still getting lost or clicking the wrong things or being frustrated, but your product is also getting bigger!

Good designs solve many symptoms and treat the causes of those symptoms, so you get more value with *fewer* changes and features, and the product becomes *less* complex over time, from a user perspective.

If you find yourself doing a lot of small design tasks, and staying very busy, but without making a lot of progress for the product as a whole, you might be treating symptoms instead of causes.

Start with research!

You Can Have Too Much Empathy

A lot of people get into UX to *help users*. That's a great motivation and perspective on the whole design process, so no complaints there. But with empathy, it is definitely possible to have too much of a good thing.

You help users most by designing excellent solutions to their problems, but those solutions will not always look like what users have requested, and sometimes users will ask for things that actually make their own experience more dangerous!

Users tend to ask for small, fairly obvious features, like "I wish I could link directly from here to there." If you built all of those little requests for all of the users that mention them, your product might be chaos! And often the value of each request is very small in the big picture.

Treat user feedback as *symptoms*, not possible *features*. Find the root causes that make users feel that way and solve it for real. Maybe they want that link "from here to there" because the navigation is confusing!

If you are a shy person or just insecure about your place in the design world, you might go to user feedback as a safe way to make decisions. But when you start to *obey users*, you are not the expert anymore, and your value as a designer is much lower.

And what if a user wants an easier way to do something dangerous, like deleting their account?! Probabilities are more important than user requests. If you make it easier to delete their account, you also make it easier to delete an account *by mistake*! So, one user's request is another user's big mistake.

But if that feature is created, it won't matter *who* caused all of those deleted accounts.

Value, diagnostics, and probabilities are not based on empathy. Empathy is just a good way to align yourself—emotionally—with your users. And that's where it should stop.

"A Paying Customer Wants a Stupid Feature. What Should We Do?"

Officially, the answer to this question is the same as the previous section. But instead of empathy (a noble force in the universe and therefore no concern to most companies) motivating you then, *money* is the motivation now. Suddenly the *business* has an opinion about which features you have to make and everybody is afraid to say no and thinks the situation has changed.

It hasn't. But it *is* harder *politically* to make the smart choice.

I have worked in several companies with big, rich enterprise customers. Some of them react quickly and change their plans immediately when customers have any request at all, and some of them say, "We will consider it for future road map planning and let you know if we decide to build it."

The first type of company always runs around like crazy people, constantly changing plans and building features whether any other customer wants them or not, and their products are invariably a mess. The second type of company fits in as many requested features as they can, and *very* occasionally makes an exception for requests that are especially valuable to customers, but generally just keeps on keepin' on, managing their product road map like professionals.

The real irony, though? The first type of company, which is constantly granting customer wishes, is often treated poorly by those same customers! Most people think the second type of company would just be annoying all of their customers, but the opposite is true! And since the first type is always treated badly, they become more and more afraid of saying no.

In real life, if you teach customers that wishes will always be granted ASAP, you will become *less* valuable in their eyes, as a product and as a company! They feel like they can control you. But if you have your own plans, carefully considered and well managed, customers will learn to respect you instead and look forward to the solutions you deliver, requested or not. It will seem like a *favor* when you prioritize a customer request instead of a desperate rush to make them happy.

Pragmatism Should Always Win

For some people, especially at a senior level, there is an *intellectual* quality to design. I appreciate the intellectual design conversation, but in practice, at work, with real users and limitations, intellectual priorities usually lead to bad decisions.

Intellectual priorities come in many forms, and one form is the idea of "purity."

When we learned about *strategic inconsistency* earlier, we were breaking the principle of purity that some people care about a lot. Your Android and iPhone apps *should* (usually) look a little different! They are different operating systems, and users have different expectations about where navigation should be, etc.

But when an intellectual developer, for example, starts to argue that the code base would be easier to maintain if both apps were identical, and it would be more "pure" if we had a single design to rule them all...this intellectual principle of "purity" might feel very persuasive.

When designing a business in the real world for real users, *pragmatism*, or the idea of solving a problem in the most practical way (rather than theoretically), should win. Slightly different apps will *work* better in reality, even if they are "less pure" theoretically.

Another form of purity is when designers want to design for *every* use case instead of the use cases that are relevant or important. For example, I have had an argument that we should allow blog posts to have a headline that is a million characters long, because "users might want that." Or we could limit the headline to a few hundred characters and avoid all of these theoretical, but totally impractical, scenarios.

As a designer, you have the power to help bad choices happen. If you avoid conflict and just say, "Yeah, that makes sense, I guess," then *you allow* a blog layout for an infinitely long headline. What would that even look like? Insane, probably. But since you avoided the argument instead of taking the pragmatic path (limiting headline length to a reasonable number of characters), now *you* have to design that solution.

Maybe a user will want that someday. Kill it anyway.

No Research and No Strategy = Random Decisions

It is sad, but true, that a lot of companies don't really have a strategy. They are doing precisely what their competitors are doing, in roughly the same way, and expecting superior results for some reason. In bigger companies, or in teams of people who have worked in the same place for a long time, they might not know what they contribute to the company; they just follow the routines they have always followed.

Like I said, sad, but true.

If you work in a company with a weak strategy, hope is not lost! With good research and a VDP approach, the product team can drag the company in a good direction by doing good work. Be the change you want to see in the world, and all that.

However, the worst-case scenario is that you don't have a good strategy *and* you don't base product decisions on user research or data. That product and that company are just drifting on the ocean, and eventually they will be eaten by a competitor shark.

If you work somewhere like that, you have two choices: either you turn things around and get your team to start doing research and planning a good road map based on a VDP approach, or you go work somewhere else.

Hard? Yes. Impossible? No.

Without strategy and without research you are not building a product or service, you are just pretending to be busy while you get a paycheck. On the other hand, if that sounds good to you, you might be in the right place!

Design Like You Own the Place

In this last section of the book, I want to recommend the opposite of just going to work and collecting your paycheck.

The best results I have achieved in my career were usually when I was given responsibility and the bosses were too busy to check on me for a while. When they looked, I had run so far with the work, the original goals weren't enough anymore.

If there isn't a strategy, make one. If there isn't research, start some. And if you're not "allowed," find a way to do it anyway. Recruit a few colleagues! In the old days that was called a "skunk works" project. Don't take risks that might kill the company, but *do* take creative risks!

Make prototypes without asking, talk to users whenever you can, propose things that are ambitious, and *actively try* to be the first in the world to solve a valuable problem. Act like the company might die without you, and time is running out!

There has been a trend over the past 10 years of people doing more "fake it till you make it" than actually making it. Design theater, I call it. Workshops that achieve nothing, hackathons and internal projects to look good on LinkedIn, and eight-word job titles that are all fluff, to name a few examples. "All hat and no cattle," as they would say in Texas.

Don't design to look good. Definitely don't design like you're afraid to color outside the lines. If something doesn't work, try to fix it! Founders don't ask for permission; they get shit done. It is better to try 10 things that don't work on the way to a great solution than to do 10 safe things and never make anything valuable.

Many, many, many designers want someone to tell them what to do. Bosses, users, competitors, whoever. But the best designers *hunt* for valuable problems to solve, like user value is what they eat.

If you sit and wait for food, you will starve. But if you become a good hunter, you will always be happy.

Index

About the Author

Joel Marsh is the founder of Peekerton, a company that does confidential user experience analysis and design for high-value clients like global private equity investors, new corporate ventures, and strategic agencies. As a UX Architect, his work represents hundreds of millions of users and billions of dollars in investments, including some of the most famous companies in the world.

Colophon

The cover design and original cover art are by Susan Thompson. The cover fonts are Guardian Sans and Gilroy Semibold. The text fonts are Scala Pro, Benton Sans, and Minion Pro; the heading font is Benton Sans; and the code font is Ubuntu Mono.

Printed in the USA
CPSIA information can be obtained
at www.ICGtesting.com
JSHW011226091223
53546JS00003B/37

9 781098 110598